A Collectors
COLOUR
HOME SWEET HOME
AND OTHER COLLECTIONS

John Hughes

Published in the United Kingdom
by
Collectables Publishing Limited

ACKNOWLEDGMENTS

Many thanks to the following people:
Frances and Peter Fagan for their cooperation and enthusiasm
for the project, for permission to reproduce copyright text
from a variety of printed sources, and for proofing
and correcting the manuscript;
Everyone at Bronze Age Limited who provided information,
in particular Liz Bernard, Pam Ellison, Terry Fairbairn, Pat Glass,
Hazel Gryczka, Pat Learmonth, Margaret Smith and
Joan Walker-Alton;
Penny Davies of Ronn Ballantyne Photographic for extensive
use of existing photography;
Glenn Blackman for design and original photography;
Myra Whellans for details about the early days at Bronze Age Limited;
The numerous collectors and dealers who provided
information — Roger Boylan, Kathleen Cook, Lynda Gould,
the Marks family, Morna Reeves, Arild Soloest, Carrie Sterk, Neil at
Lynn's Cards and Gifts in Woking,
and especially Ann Macfarlane.

Thanks also to Peter Gilardi of The Grange, Lauder.

Front cover picture:
The original painting master of Moonlight Serenade

The information in this book was compiled as accurately as possible at the time of going to print. Please note that prices, names and other factual information, especially relating to new products, are subject to change.

ISBN 0 9522155 4 3

© 1995 Collectables Publishing Limited
3 East Street, Littlehampton,
West Sussex, BN17 6AU England
Telephone: (01903) 733199 Fax: (01903) 733244

Produced by Creativehouse, Aldershot.

Introduction

Colour Box miniatures were created in 1983 out of necessity. For ten years Peter Fagan had been running a modest craft company — Bronze Age Limited — based in the quiet Scottish Border town of Lauder, where he employed a handful of local people. He sculpted, cast and sold a range of cold cast bronzes (animal figurines, lamp stands etc.).

But by the early 1980s the future for bronzes was not looking rosy and Peter realised that a change in direction was required. So one day he took a bronze miniature of a cat and painted it, thus adding both colour and humour. The response from his customers was extraordinary — the new style sold like hotcakes. In a short space of time production of bronzes was replaced by hand painted ceramic resin miniatures and Peter had found his new direction.

It was something of a rebirth. From that point onwards Bronze Age Limited, using a new trading name, 'Colour Box', to reflect the new colourful image, started to grow. From a parochial craft company it gradually metamorphosed into a major giftware and collectable company, with a small army of employees producing tens of thousands of miniatures every week to satisfy a worldwide demand for sculptures by Peter Fagan.

So what happened? Where lies the secret of this sudden success? *Colour* was the key that unlocked the Colour Box, certainly, but it also unleashed qualities within Peter's work which had not been fully realised before — a nostalgia for childhood days, an impish sense of humour. These ingredients, combined with the ever popular subject of animals (cats in particular) made Home Sweet Home and Hopscotch two winning collections. Four years later the same appeal brought even greater success with the Teddy Bear Collection.

Peter understands collectors because he is a collector himself. His home is filled with all sorts of memorabilia and curios and the thought of an afternoon spent wandering in and out of antique shops attracts him greatly. This romantic attachment to things of the past he communicates through his models.

Affordability, too, has played an important role. Many of Peter Fagan's miniatures can be purchased at pocket money prices, which is more than can be said of most collectable ranges in the 1990s. No wonder the Colour Box Collectors Club has a high number of children amongst its members and that many children of a decade ago are today still eager collectors in their teens and early twenties.

Then there is the sheer appeal of Peter's work, the intangible, the image that creates an emotional response. His pieces make you smile, they remind you of your own childhood — not an idealistic memory, but how things really were, with milk bottles knocked over on the doorstep, clothes hanging from a drawer, furniture chipped and damaged, teddy bears hugged out of shape and with fur worn away.

Whatever the reasons, Peter Fagan's Colour Box miniatures are one of the most popular collectables around and Peter one of the most prolific artists. Since colour superseded bronze, he has sculpted over 700 figurines and around 30 million miniatures have left the Scottish Borders, every one hand cast and hand painted. The time has come for a catalogue of his work!

In two volumes — *A Collectors Guide to Colour Box Teddy Bears* and *A Collectors Guide to Colour Box Home Sweet Home and Other Collections* — I have attempted to list every miniature (current and retired) ever produced under the Colour Box name, plus details of manufacture, painting and mould variations, colourways, rare and unreleased items, Colour Box memorabilia and a secondary market price guide. In other words, everything you could possibly need to know about Colour Box. I may or may not have succeeded; it's difficult to tell with an artist as prolific as Peter Fagan as there may always be some forgotten piece lurking in a collection somewhere waiting to be catalogued.

The information contained herein has been compiled with the full cooperation of Bronze Age Limited and Frances and Peter Fagan in particular, the finer points being honed during two weeks of research in Lauder. Some of my time there was spent in jail . . . read on!

John Hughes
February 1995

About the Author

John Hughes was born in 1956 in Sutton Coldfield, West Midlands. He trained as a classical musician and gained an honours degree from London University in 1977. He then spent a number of years in music retailing, working for Harrods and Yamaha, during which time his first book — *Keyboard Magic* — was published by A & C Black. In 1985 he joined John Hine Limited, makers of David Winter Cottages, initially to develop a music recording branch of the company. But he very soon found himself side-stepping into the world of collectables and giftware and for the next eight years was involved in establishing and developing the David Winter Collectors Guild. In 1993 he left John Hine Limited and, together with Heather Lavender, established Collectables Publishing Limited (CPL) to produce books about collectable ranges. It was then that he became aware of the collectability of Colour Box and acquired his first piece — August String-Bear. In 1994 he and Heather approached Peter Fagan with a view to collaborating on a book about Colour Box. Such was Peter's enthusiasm for the project that six months later the two volumes were complete. John currently has seven published books to his credit (plus an unpublished novel!). He lives in Surrey with his wife, Chris, and daughters, Helen and Alice. In his spare time he enjoys listening to, and occasionally composing, music.

Contents

Acknowledgments	ii
Introduction	iii
About the Author	iv
Contents	v

Section One

THE COLOUR BOX STORY	6
COLLECTING COLOUR BOX	10

Section Two

HOME SWEET HOME	18
PERSONALITY PUPS	59
MINIATURE COLLECTION	66
HOPSCOTCH MINIS	72
PENNYWHISTLE LANE	82
COLOUR BOX IN THE USA	92
THE COLLECTORS CLUB	95
LIMITED EDITIONS	100
OTHER ITEMS	
Arthur the Cat Collection	102
Good Golly	103
SEASONAL COLLECTION	109

Section Three

RARE AND UNRELEASED ITEMS	113
MEMORABILIA	116
SECONDARY MARKET PRICE GUIDE	120
INDEX	127

The Colour Box Story

The Colour Box story is primarily the story of one man, sculptor Peter Fagan. He was born on 5th November 1942. His father was from Galway on the West Coast of Ireland and his mother's family stems from Scotland, but despite these deeply Celtic roots Peter was actually born and bred in Essex. It was there, on the lower edge of East Anglia, that he spent his formative years and where many of the people, places and things existed that were to inspire Home Sweet Home, the first Colour Box collection, some thirty years later.

Peter was the artist of the family (he is the eldest of five children) and his ability was apparent at a very early age. His first school report, when he was five, said that he was *"excellent in plasticine and should do well with his modelling."* — prophetic words, and to this day Peter still uses plasticine to create his original figurines.

On graduating from Colchester College of Art in the early 1960s, Peter tried his hand at a number of jobs, beginning with a stint as a bus conductor (*"an excellent cure for shyness,"* he says!). Then he taught pottery at Braintree College of Further Education and worked as an assistant in an art studio where, amongst other prestigious commissions, he was responsible for casting the avante-garde bronze sculptures in Coventry Cathedral. At that time he also produced a great many relief panels.

One day he saw a vacancy advertised for an exhibition stand designer with a large company. Despite lacking any experience, Peter applied and managed to talk himself into the job. For a number of years he worked on exhibitions both in the UK and abroad, and when he left the company, he then fulfilled several large commissions for theatres, prestige offices and a church.

At this point in his career Peter felt the need for a completely fresh start. So in 1972, with no specific plans in mind, he sold his house and drove up to Scotland where he had once spent an enjoyable holiday. After several weeks touring around, and looking at properties in the Highlands, he eventually moved back further south to the Borders. *"I ran out of petrol in Lauder,"* he says, *"and there I stayed."*

That was on a Friday. At 7.30am the next morning he awoke to the sound of a brass band, horses' hooves and whisky toasts in the street outside! He had arrived just in time to witness the Lauder Common Riding, an ancient traditional ceremony in which local people ride around the boundaries of the town to ensure that adjoining landowners have not encroached upon the "Common Lands of the Burgh."

To pay the bills, Peter got a job in a local factory and began taking private commissions, primarily making relief plaques — clan crests, coats of arms — and even pub signs. Living in a house on the High Street, he had some of his plaques on display in The Eagle Hotel a few yards down the road, and well remembers on occasions taking orders in the bar then rushing home to make the plaques! Some of his work from this period can still be seen in and around Lauder. Most notable are four coats of arms in Lauder church, sculpted to celebrate its tercentenary in November 1973.

Earlier the same year Peter had wandered into a craft shop and seen some figurines of owls made in cold cast bronze resin. He thought to himself, *"I can do that,"* and promptly went home and set to work. In a short time he had modelled, cast and polished a selection of animal figurines and was soon doing the rounds of local shops with a bag full of pieces. *"If the shopkeepers didn't like them,"* he recalls, *" I'd pretend I hadn't made them and even offer to take*

Before Colour Box there was Bronze Age. Left: A selection of Peter Fagan's animal figurines in cold cast bronze. Far left: Peter at work in his Lauder studio in the 1970s.

back their critical comments to the artist, promising better next time!" But enough shopkeepers did like them for a business to materialise and in 1973 Bronze Age Limited was established.

Production took place initially in and around Peter's house in Lauder — 11 West High Street — with people working in different rooms. His first employee was Myra Whellans. "I worked in the little bedroom at Granny Baxter's," she remembers (Granny Baxter owned the house before Peter). Business gradually developed and by 1975 the company employed ten people. "Peter was sculpting in another bedroom," Myra says, "there were polishers in the kitchen and casting was done in the loft of the old stable belonging to the grocer. Then eventually I moved into the jail!"

Lauder jail consists of three cells under the Town Hall; two with small grated windows and one (called the 'Black Hole') without any window at all. Its use as a jail was discontinued in 1843, and when Peter Fagan first rented it in the 1970s he used one cell as a shop, the other (where Myra worked) as a packing room and the Black Hole for storage. Myra remembers an American arriving one day and asking for Peter. She directed him to 'Granny Baxter's' in the High Street; and it was thus that Bronze Age received their first order for the USA.

The next move was to one of three workshop units on the town's Orchard Estate (known as 'top factory') and in time the company has expanded into all three. By the end of the 1970s the product range had also expanded: animal figurines varying from large prestige pieces such as a Welsh Cob to a collection of tiny ones called 'Tiddlers'; there were also plaques, lamp stands and paperweights.

By the early 1980s, however, it was clear to Peter Fagan that interest in bronze figurines was waning. He also felt that artistically he had done all he could within the medium. So in late 1982, as an experiment, he took a small bronze figurine of a cat and painted it. *"The response was extraordinary,"* he says. *"It sold like wildfire."* Soon the Hopscotch range of miniature painted animals appeared and within a few months they were generating a quarter of Bronze Age Limited's turnover. Other bronze sculptures were adapted to create the Miniature Collection.

Clearly this was the way of the future and Peter proceeded to re-think the entire product range. He changed from using cold cast resin to a ceramic resin and employed hand painters to create warm, natural colours on the pieces. Then he worked on the idea of placing the highly popular cat models into different situations, combining humour with nostalgia. His first notion was of a cat foraging in a dustbin for food, and this became Trash Can Cat, the very first Home Sweet Home piece to be sculpted.

Calling upon his past and happy boyhood memories, Peter gradually developed a collection. In those days he had a primitive but effective means of market research; place sculptures in the front window of his house in Lauder High Street and see what people's reactions were. Passers-by were soon knocking on the door and asking about the funny cat models, and this positive sign was cemented by the hundreds of orders from shops that came flooding in after the first showing of the pieces at the Spring Trade

7

Fair in early 1983. Home Sweet Home was a great success from the start. Bronze sculptures were abandoned.

It was in 1983 that Peter also devised a name to reflect the move towards more colourful models. He chose 'Colour Box' to suggest his own old paint box and the fact that each piece is hand painted. 'Colour Box' is a trading name, but to this day Peter has never changed the company name which still remains Bronze Age Limited. However, in the same year an American distributor was appointed and for the USA the name 'Adorables' was chosen instead of 'Colour Box.'

During the mid 1980s Home Sweet Home went from strength to strength whilst other collections fell by the wayside and were retired (Baby Animals, The Mutts). Then in 1987 Peter was on holiday in Belgium with his wife Frances. One wet afternoon in Bruges they took shelter in an old curios shop and there amongst the bric-a-brac he spied a number of old teddy bears — four in all. He purchased three of them (soon to be christened Robert, Peregrine and August String Bear) and after a sleepless night of regret at leaving the fourth, went back the next day for Gustav von Bruin. With the names came imaginary histories which the Fagans devised together and Frances wrote down, and in Peter's mind the idea for a new collection began to formulate.

The Teddy Bear Collection was launched the following year (1988), and Peter found himself with a success on his hands to rival that of Home Sweet Home. As a setting for the bears he sculpted a model of the curios shop in Bruges where the idea had originated and on a return visit discovered yet another bear for the collection — Johann. More real bears were acquired, mainly from auction rooms, and as the Fagans' own collection developed so too did the range of sculptures (40 pieces in the first three years), often with a familiar bear placed in an amusing or nostalgic setting. That every new bear in the range is a sculpture of a real bear owned by Peter and Frances has remained a unifying factor throughout. It has also been Peter's inspiration. He says: *"The attraction to me of the real bears is that they belonged to someone and are therefore part of them, and that's what I try to capture."*

The arrival of teddy bears coincided with the launch of the Colour Box Collectors Club in June 1987. This was well received by collectors for two reasons: first because a regular Club newsletter provided them with much needed news and information about their collections; secondly, Peter Fagan started sculpting special pieces available exclusively for Club members. Within three years there were 10,000 members and by the end of 1994 Colour Box had recruited more than 40,000 in seven years.

Frances Fagan had been helping with the Collectors Club newsletter from the beginning by writing articles and answering letters. In 1989 she became full time editor and has been the driving force behind the Club ever since. She has also skillfully created storylines for the bears that she and Peter have adopted and named (if their history isn't already known).

On July 8 1989 the Colour Box shop and visitors centre was opened in the Old Smiddy, the oldest building in Lauder and, coincidentally, almost opposite the jail where Myra Whellans used to work (and which to this day still houses the Colour Box archives). The shop has always been run by Pat Learmonth who has welcomed a continuous stream of visitors ever since.

In the 1990s the popularity of the Teddy Bear Collection has increased considerably, and so has the collection. One of the prime sources for new bears has been Christie's in London and the Fagans have become familiar faces in the famous auction rooms whenever teddies are featured in the catalogue. When Christie's first ever sale devoted entirely to teddy bears was held on 6th December 1993, Peter and Frances reciprocated by donating 40 lots, the proceeds of which went to charity (Child Accident Prevention Trust). The lots included the masters of some of Peter's sculptures, real plush covered teddy bears and all ten of a limited edition piece sculpted specially for the occasion — The Auction Room. This event more than anything established Colour Box as highly collectable, if there was ever any doubt!

As well as the main collections, Colour Box have, in recent years, established a portfolio of additional prestigious work — the Edward Harrod, Lawleys, Hermann and Steiff collections, plus pieces for British Airways, Barclaycard Profiles and other commissions. As well as the Christie's sale, the Fagans have also regularly generated projects to raise money for selected charities, usually involving the donation of profits from the sale of pieces (e.g. Cat Napper, Teddy Randell, Safety Ted, Teddy Royale).

Peter Fagan has always been one for trying new ventures and with Home Sweet Home and Teddy Bears as the two main ranges, he has produced a number of projects which have met with varying degrees of success: Tableaux, Celebration Cakes, Menus, Early Days, Town and Country Collection. In the case of the last two, he encountered the problem of promoting sculptures which were 'Colour Box' but not 'Peter Fagan' and in the eyes of ardent collectors the two were (and still are) synonymous. To bypass this problem, in 1990 he established Cavalcade, a sister company to run parallel with Colour Box and to promote the work of other artists. Collections marketed under the Cavalcade name consist of: Bear Facts, Beasties of the Kingdom, The Bogeymen, British Blighters, Bugs Bunny and Friends, The Cheddars, The Class, Dragon Keep, Eggbert and Friends, Fairweather, The Herd, In the Doghouse, Mr Stubbs, Secrets of the Forest, Perrfect Pets, Whiskers Cats and Dogs, and the World of Krystonia.

1994 saw the launch of a number of new Colour Box collections — Pennywhistle Lane, Good Golly, Arthur the Cat. Of specific interest is Pennywhistle Lane as it represents an entirely new concept for a collection; not just cats or bears but a selection of characters and items (including a whole family of mice) that inhabit the loft of a house.

In the USA Pennywhistle Lane is currently used as an umbrella title for a collection of pieces selected from all the Colour Box ranges being distributed by the Enesco Corporation, and replaces the 'Adorables' range. However, Teddies are also available as a separate collection under the name 'Centimental Bears'. Home Sweet Home cats are due to be launched under their own range name in 1996.

The connection with Enesco is one of a number of projects which will lead Peter Fagan and Bronze Age Limited into exciting new directions during the second half of the 1990s. The other important change is the amalgamation in 1995 of Colour Box and Cavalcade under one name: Colour Box — The World of Peter Fagan. Thus Peter's work and that of other artists will all be identified as the product of Colour Box studios, including The Herd and Eggbert and Friends from the Cavalcade collections, plus new ranges such as Lakeland Bears and Little Darlings.

Colour Box is a delightful success story. It started with a few sculptures sold from a bag and is currently a multi-million marketing concern. In twelve years Peter Fagan has created over 700 miniatures and his work can be bought in as many as 35 countries worldwide.

And the Colour Box story continues . . .

Collecting Colour Box

HOW COLOUR BOX FIGURINES ARE MADE

SCULPTING When sculpting Peter Fagan works from home in an attic studio overlooking the beautiful Tweed river. His raw material is plasticine and an original model he creates is always the same size as the final painted piece which a collector buys. To achieve the fine detail on his work he uses an array of small modelling tools, plus anything suitable for the purpose, including dental equipment, hat pins and embroidery utensils. He once scoured every junk shop in the Borders for a tea strainer fine enough to create the texture of the poodle wool on the Frou Frou's!

"I find it hard to get started sometimes," he admits, "but I'm alright once I get going. I listen to the radio as I work — Radio 4 usually. Some pieces come quicker than others and, surprisingly, it's often the quicker ones that tend to work better as far as I am concerned and also become more popular with collectors. Cats are more difficult to sculpt than teddy bears because although we own three cats of our own, I'm not sculpting an exact model every time. Having done so many models now I need to use source material than I used to — books, periodicals. I'm also more precise these days. For example, if I'm sculpting a drawer I will construct it like a carpenter would, assembling each piece with dovetail joints. Then if it needs to look like an old drawer I'll 'distress' it. I didn't take so much care with the earlier models and now I'm embarrassed when I look at them!

"Sculpturally I 'build' rather than 'cut away'. In other words I don't start with a large block and chisel away at it; I prefer to assemble pieces bit by bit, as with the drawer. This applies to large or small pieces, and in fact large pieces are an assembly of lots of small pieces, if you think about it."

When a model is finished, it is kept cold in a freezer so the plasticine is not easily damaged or distorted, and then taken to the mould makers at the 'top factory' in Lauder.

MOULD MAKING To create a master mould Peter's plasticine original is first surrounded by four walls of cardboard. Liquid silicon rubber is then poured over it until the plasticine is fully submerged. When the rubber has set the plasticine is removed from the space it has left inside the rubber block leaving a perfect mould of Peter's original (which is destroyed in the process). From this block mould a number of 'copies' of Peter's original are cast in tough, durable green resin ('greenware'). The quantity depends on the size of the piece: a large piece may have less than ten production masters, whereas smaller pieces have thirty or more. The masters can be used to make more moulds of the same piece, and by doing so Peter's original can be duplicated in large numbers.

CASTING, GRINDING AND FETTLING In the casting shop, the moulds are filled with a liquid mixture of ceramic and resin which, with the aid of a slow trip through an oven, sets hard in under two hours. Still warm, the pieces are carefully removed from the moulds, then taken in trays to have the bases trimmed flat. This is done using high speed circular grinders. The 'whiteware' (as unpainted pieces are called) is then 'fettled' — flashes of excess ceramic which sometimes occur during casting are removed using dental burrs. After fettling the pieces are wash-sprayed in a liquid not unlike nail varnish and then dried in preparation for painting.

PAINTING Colour Box miniatures are painted primarily by outworkers who collect whiteware from a number of 'stations' dotted around the Borders region, paint the pieces at home and return them when complete. There are also two workshops (at Haddington and Berwick upon Tweed) where painting is done 'in-house'. Before being let loose, however, painters must undergo intensive training from skilled Colour Box tutors on a one-to-one basis, and even then it may take up to three years before they can tackle the more difficult sculptures. Painting time varies enormously:

Far left: Peter sculpting an original master in plasticine. Left: Block moulds being filled with a liquid mixture of ceramic and resin. Below: Dental burrs are used to 'fettle' away excess material.

a Hopscotch miniature may take just a few minutes, but something like Moonlight Serenade can keep even the most experienced Colour Box painter occupied for up to six hours.

At one time the colours for a new piece were originated by Peter himself, but for a number of years this has been the task of Terry Fairbairn. She has more than 250 standard colours to choose from and can spend several days working on one piece. When they first started working together Peter used to brief her about the colours he had in mind, but nowadays there is no need as they are so much on the same wavelength that Terry invariably gets it right first time.

PACKING AND DESPATCH Painted pieces are then finished by adding velour (larger pieces only) and a label and then wrapping and boxing them ready for despatch to shops worldwide.

VARIATIONS AND COLOURWAYS

Occasionally, though rarely, a Colour Box miniature is altered after it has been released. This is done by modifying a 'master' and making new moulds. In this book these are called Mould Variations — the original is called 'Mould 1' and the modified version 'Mould 2'. When such a change is made, the original version (Mould 1) becomes retired and acquires a secondary market value, effectively as a 'limited edition' of unknown number — even if the Mould 2 version is still currently available. Some variations can be very slight (e.g. Just Good Friends) whilst others are more apparent (Yuletide). All known mould variations are itemised in Section Two as part of the information about individual pieces.

Far more common, however, are variations to the colours of pieces. These exist for a number of reasons:
1) A conscious decision by Colour Box to change the colours during production (e.g. Lamp, Flat Cap).
2) Slight differences between the work of individual painters.
3) Deliberately modified versions of a piece (called 'colourways' or 'paintways') created in limited numbers for a special event, such as a store promotion or charity (e.g. All Lit Up, Peaceful Pup).

Colour Box do not possess definitive records of mould or colour variations. All available information is listed in Section Two, and this has been enhanced by details of pieces in individual collections. But further variations are bound to exist.

Right: A selection of early pieces with the original Home Sweet Home boxes which Colour Box used until the late 1980s. Far right: From top to bottom, examples of an early, middle and late base label.

CODE NUMBERS

Within certain collections (Home Sweet Home, Hopscotch) it may appear that the code numbers of some figurines have been duplicated. In fact Colour Box occasionally reallocate numbers from retired pieces to new ones (e.g. Festive Fun, Bright and Early - both HS319) and rarely are two figurines with the same number both current at the same time. Exceptions are: Home Sweet Home — Piano Pops and Washtand, both HS213 and current together between 1988 and 1992. One number — H16 in the Hopscotch collection — has been used three times (Snake, Lion, Mouse).

Generally speaking the first digit of a code number in the Home Sweet Home collection identifies the price band of the piece, and the higher the number the lower the value. This has not been adhered to strictly over the years and there are many exceptions. Also pieces such as Limited Editions do not apply.

Colour Box sculptures and memorabilia code numbers are prefixed by the following letters:
BK = Books, CA = Arthur (also used for Cards), CC = Collectors Club (since 1993),
CM = Ceramics, DG = Personality Pups,
GG = Good Golly, H = Hopscotch,
HS = Home Sweet Home, MC = Miniature Collection, PL = Pennywhistle Lane,
PS = Pictures,
TC = Teddy Bears, XHS / XTC = Christmas Collection.

BOXES AND PACKAGING

Between 1983 and 1989 Colour Box miniatures were supplied in white boxes (assorted sizes) with brown illustrations of a cottage exterior: the top of the box was sloped like a roof and the front face was removable. The main text reads: 'Colour Box Miniatures.' In 1989 these were replaced by the red, green and blue boxes in various sizes which are still current in 1995 and at the same time the new 'Colour Box' logo was also created. Yellow boxes were also introduced for the Miniature Collection. Both the boxes and the logo were designed to reflect the 'Colour Box' name. Prior to the introduction of the new boxes, Teddies were issued in plain pink boxes with a Colour Box sticker attached. Inside all boxes the packaging has always consisted of either tissue paper or 'bubble-wrap'.

Prestige limited edition pieces (e.g. Moonlight Serenade) are presented in customised silk-lined boxes.

STORY LEAFLETS

Stories have always been an important part of the Teddy Bear Collection and every bear is accompanied by his own story leaflet, written by Frances Fagan. This also applies to Pennywhistle Lane but not to the Hopscotch, Personality Pups or Miniature collections. The stories are sometimes true, sometimes imaginary, and sometimes a blend of the two. On several fictional storylines have turned out to be uncannily accurate, to Frances' astonishment (e.g. Martin, Binkie, Teddy Randell, Teddy Robinson). Traditionally Home Sweet Home have not had story leaflets, but eight were introduced in 1994 to see if collectors would like them, and more may follow. The eight pieces are: Piano Pops, Cat's Chorus, Afternoon Stroll, The Correspondent, Milk Churns, Upstairs-Downstairs, Wakey Wakey and Fishbowl. The inspiration and stories behind others appear regularly in the Collectors Club magazine, Collections & Reflections.

CATS

Some but by no means all of the cats on Home Sweet Home sculptures are in fact characters from the Hopscotch collection and they recur frequently on a number of pieces — Striped Cat (H1), Plain Cat (H2), Black Cat (H10) are all regulars. Others are sculpted afresh by Peter Fagan. Occasionally the type of cat may be changed during production; this can be useful in distinguishing an early version of a piece from a later one. For example, Welsh Dresser (HS211) originally featured a ginger Striped Cat (H1), but on later pieces it became Big Black Cat (H42). Known changes are recorded under the individual headings of pieces in Section Two, although the list does not claim to be definitive.

LABELS AND VELOUR

LABELS The paper labels (sometimes called 'backstamps') to be found on the base of all but the tiniest pieces. They have varied slightly over the years and this can be useful in identifying the approximate production date of a piece. All Colour Box labels are blue and circular, but . . .
EARLY LABELS (1983 - 1986) state only: *Made and Hand Painted in Scotland.*
MIDDLE LABELS (1986 - 1992) state: *Made and Hand Painted in Scotland* plus Peter Fagan's signature and the year of issue.
RECENT LABELS (1993 onwards) state the name of the piece, a copyright symbol, the date of issue, the code number of the piece, but not the country of origin: e.g. *Upstairs Downstairs   Peter Fagan © 1994   HS806.*
Consequently a piece such as The Wall, sculpted in 1983 and retired in 1985, will only be found with an early label (and on occasions no label at all), whilst Kitchen Range, issued in 1983 and retired only in 1995, may be found with all three types of label.
Although the stickiness of labels fades with time and labels sometimes fall off, every effort should be made to reattach them, as labels provide authenticity as well as factual information.

VELOUR   Velour is attached to the base of larger miniatures but not smaller ones. By far the most common colour of the velour is red, although other colours are used from time to time. There is a very good practical reason for this: sometimes the village store in Lauder runs out of red velour!
In 1994 velour cut to the shape of a piece and covering the entire base was replaced by a number of small velour discs dotted across the base.

MARKINGS

The markings on Peter Fagan's sculptures vary considerably, from a simple touchmark (PF) to a complete signature, copyright symbol (©) and date — or any combination of these ingredients. Some pieces have no markings at all. During 1992 he used a stamp in the shape of a rosette to emboss the words HAND PAINTED and his signature, but the text was difficult to read and its use was discontinued. The rosette can be seen on some but not all 1992 releases (e.g. Klim, Benji, Prudence, Grand Prix Ted, Miranda, Jerome [Teddies] — Early Bloomers, The Groundsman, The Last Drop [Home Sweet Home]). Location of the markings also varies but they are always to be found on the visible faces, never on the base.

THE SECONDARY MARKET

When Bronze Age Limited produce a piece, they supply quantities to their authorised stockists (shops) who then sell them to their customers. This is called the 'primary market'. When the company chooses to discontinue (or 'retire') production of a piece, and once existing stocks have been sold, the piece will no longer be available from their stockists. The only way then to acquire the piece is either from another collector or from a dealer who specialises in the buying

Right: Spot the difference! Three versions of Just Good Friends (HS534), one without a bow (left), one with a bow painted on freehand (centre), and the 'Mould 2' version with the bow sculpted on and painted (right).

and selling of retired pieces. This is called the 'secondary market'.

When a regular figurine is retired it in effect becomes a 'limited edition', by virtue of the fact that it is no longer produced; this applies even though the edition size remains unknown. As a result, demand for the piece (and therefore its monetary value) increases. Ironically the most common reason for retiring a piece is that it has lost its appeal and is not selling well; but once it is retired, the opposite invariably applies.

The rate at which a piece increases in value depends upon its rarity value; the longer the production run the smaller the demand. For example, High Noon and Midnight Cat were only produced between 1983 and 1986, whereas Gang's Chair, also issued in 1983, was in production for a decade.

Colourways produced for a special promotion or event are very collectable as the number produced are usually quite limited. Serious collectors will often want to acquire every colourway version of the same piece and therefore pay premium prices on the secondary market.

Most collectable of all are the relatively few pieces produced in pre-announced, numbered limited editions (e.g. Moonlight Serenade [1,500]). Although more expensive initially, these are the figurines which will increase in value the most over a period of time.

Collectors for whom investment is a consideration should also be aware of the attraction of the Colour Box Collectors Club pieces. Not only is availability limited by time (usually one year) but also by number (total Club membership), and in the case of Club offers the percentage of Club members who choose to purchase the piece. These restrictions give them a collectability second only to numbered limited editions.

PLEASE NOTE It is important to point out that the buying and selling of retired pieces is carried out independently of Bronze Age Limited who, as the manufacturers, rightly maintain a policy of non-involvement in the secondary market.

COUNTERFEITS

When something is collectable it also, sadly, becomes the target of counterfeiters and in this respect Colour Box miniature are on occasions no exception. Bronze Age Limited have traced replicas of their products to a number of countries including Spain, Greece, Sweden, France as well as the UK and Peter Fagan is very quick to respond in protecting his copyright, as the guilty parties have discovered to their cost! Peter has also been active in establishing the Giftware Copyright Protection Association.

From the collector's point of view there is nothing to be concerned about when buying a new labelled figurine in its box from an authorised Colour Box stockist. However, shops or individuals selling new unlabelled, unboxed pieces should be avoided and details passed onto Bronze Age Limited immediately.

Older pieces being sold on the secondary market are a different matter. People do not always keep boxes and, as mentioned earlier, labels can fall off. So when thinking of buying a piece from someone here are a few suggestions to bear in mind:

1) Always ask for the original box, packaging and leaflets.

1) Look closely for any loss of detail. Compare the piece with pictures in brochures, the Collectors Club magazines and this book.

2) Be aware of the quality of painting. Colour Box painters are thoroughly trained and quality control is high.

3) Ask questions about the piece's history. (Where did you get it from? How long have you had it?)

On the other hand, don't be over cautious! Counterfeiting is difficult, dangerous and, despite the information in this section, extremely rare.

SIGNED PIECES

Peter Fagan enjoys meeting and talking with collectors — he is after all a collector himself. He therefore regularly attends in-store promotions and special events where he signs his work. This signature is a precious addition to a piece and increases its inherent value; by how much monetarily is a very difficult question to answer, but it should be regarded as a significant advantage during resale and the vendor should be looking for a premium price. A signature should also be regarded as an indelible guarantee of authenticity.

WHERE SHOULD I BUY AND HOW MUCH SHOULD I PAY?

PRIMARY MARKET Colour Box figurines are available from Bronze Age Limited's extensive network of authorised stockists. The actual price of the pieces may vary slightly from shop to shop as stockists are not obliged to adhere to Recommended Retail Prices (indeed the company only started issuing R.R.P. lists for the first time in 1992). There are merits for shopping around, just as there are merits for establishing a good relationship with a shop which provides friendly, reliable and above all knowledgeable service.

SECONDARY MARKET There are a number of specialist dealers in retired collectables, most of whom are aware of the continuing popularity of both current and retired Colour Box figurines. For collectors wishing to purchase retired pieces they provide an excellent service. Most dealers advertise regularly in appropriate magazines and periodicals, some of which are listed in Section Three. Also, retired pieces can still be tracked down in shops at the original selling price, with a bit of time and effort.

Collectors selling pieces should bear in mind that a dealer will offer a price lower than the market value — 40% lower on average — but this fluctuates depending on circumstances, the number of pieces being sold at one time, their condition, and demand for particular pieces at the time. The importance of dealers to collectors, however, is that they have good stocks and excellent contacts with other buyers and sellers.

For collectors to acquire the full market value for their pieces, it is necessary to sell or exchange directly with other collectors. Making contact here is the problem. The classified sections of the magazines listed in Section Three is a possibility; however, word of mouth and developing contacts with other serious collectors is more desirable.

TAKING CARE OF YOUR COLLECTION

Although the ceramic/resin mix from which Colour Box miniatures are cast makes them very durable, they should nevertheless be treated with tender loving care to avoid chips and perhaps more serious damage. Should the worst happen, however, it is not necessarily the end of the world and the Colour Box Collectors Club organise a 'hospital' service. Please contact them for further information — Tel: (01578) 722780.

To dust your collection use a soft paint brush, toothbrush, make-up brush or a photographer's lens brush. For a more thorough clean, Colour Box figurines can be held briefly under a tap without effecting the paint. *BUT do not soak them in water for any length of time.*

Section Two

Introduction to Listings

All the sculptures in the collections are listed in order of code number irrespective of whether they are currently available or retired. Pieces in the Home Sweet Home collection which were never allocated code numbers can be found at the end of the list.

ISSUE AND RETIREMENT DATES

An 'Issue Date' is the year in which a particular piece was first made available for purchase by Colour Box; the season or month is also listed when known. This occasionally varies from the date marked on a figurine as Peter Fagan may have sculpted the piece in advance of its release.

A 'Retirement Date' is the year in which production of a piece ceases and it is withdrawn from the catalogue. In recent years 'retirements' have been announced in advance so that collectors have the opportunity to acquire a piece. But in the past retirements just happened if the popularity of a piece had waned.

It should be remembered that when a piece is retired it does not automatically disappear from shops. Stockists will continue to sell the piece for as long as stocks last. With a bit of detective work it is possible to track down stores who still have a piece on display at list price some considerable time after its retirement date.

ISSUE PRICES

'Issue Price' means the price for which pieces sold in shops when they were first released. This is useful information to compare with both the valuations of retired miniatures and also the most recent retail prices of current pieces.

All issue prices are intended as a guide only as individual shops are entitled to select their own selling prices. (For example, a Hopscotch piece selling in one store for £1.15 might be 99p elsewhere.) Prices between 1983 and 1991 have been reconstructed from known Colour Box trade prices and in most cases have been rounded to the nearest pound or 50p. From 1992 onwards Colour Box's Recommended Retail Price lists have been used. (The company did not issue R.R.P.s before then.)

TEXT

The text in italics narrates the inspiration and stories behind individual pieces and has been gleaned either from the story leaflets which accompany the pieces or from the Collectors Club magazine. This is primarily the work of Frances Fagan and is reproduced with her kind permission. The remaining text is factual information relating to the pieces themselves such as production variations, colourways etc.

PAINTING VARIATIONS

All Colour Box miniatures are handpainted and therefore vary slightly in colouration. It would be impossible to list every difference and the painting variations recorded in this book are primarily the known changes made by Colour Box during production. Special colourways for promotions and other events are also listed (in Section Three).

Home Sweet Home

Home Sweet Home first appeared in 1983 and the collection embodies many ideas — the warmth and gentleness to be found in a loving home, a yearning for times past, a love of feline mischievousness and, of course, fine sculpture and craftsmanship. But beware! This collection, like its creator, never takes itself too seriously. In its whimsical fashion, Home Sweet Home hopes but to raise a smile!

HOME SWEET HOME WALL

Code: HSP01
Issued: Jul 1994
Issue Price: £24.50

MILK CHURNS

If there is one place in the world where you will find Peter Fagan's cats it's anywhere where there might be a free meal! On the farm at the end of the country lane where Peter lived was a gate where the milk churns were left for collection and the local cats loved to wait in the hope that one might tip over. Occasionally they helped if a churn was wobbly, then everyone got a treat before the lorry arrived!

On early pieces (Mould 1) the piece was cast as one and the churns were hand-painted. This has now been changed and in the second version (Mould 2) the churns are cast separately, spray painted and then attached to the rest of the piece.

BEST VINTAGE

There is an enigmatic number plate on this splendid old automobile. The 'PF' isn't too difficult to guess, but the 511 is a little trickier and has been the subject of a competition in the Collectors Club magazine. Suffice to say that Peter Fagan and Guy Fawkes share something in common!

Code: HS002
Issued: Feb 1995
Issue Price: £34.50

Code: HS001
Issued: Mar 1994
Issue Price: £32.50

18

GRANNY'S DRESSER

Code: HS003
Issued: Feb 1995
Issue Price: £34.50

STAGE DOOR ▼

Code: HS011
Issued: late 1991
Retired: 1993
Issue Price: £45

What goes on behind the theatre at Pantomime time — a piece inspired by Peter's interest in his local amateur dramatic group. The brazier on this piece is a good example of a feature which had to be cast separately and then attached later to the main body of the sculpture. The piece features two Hopscotch cats — Singing Cat (H61), also cast separately, and Big Black Cat (H42).

RABBIT HUTCH

Code: HS012
Issued: late 1991
Retired: 1994
Issue Price: £30

Lucy Fagan's pet rabbit, Bigsy, was the inspiration for this piece, a place where the cats spent most of their time asleep inside on the warm straw, which Bigsey didn't seem to mind sharing!

THE HEN HOUSE

Code: HS013
Issued: late 1990
Issue Price: £30

Peter's father kept chickens. He kept them in the hen house at the bottom of the garden and called them 'his girls'. They occupied a great deal of his time and energy and also provided a continuous supply of lovely fresh eggs for breakfast. Peter has happy memories of the hen house and hilarious memories of 'Hoppy', an extraordinary one-legged cockerel who survived because they didn't have the heart to put him down when he lost his leg in an accident. Hoppy lived a long and happy life with 'the girls'.
In Colour Box's archive there is paperwork referring to this piece as The Hen Coup — presumably a working title used during pre-production. Some of the animals on this piece (two cats and the cockerel on the roof) are cast separately.

Home Sweet Home

19

THE WHEELBARROW

A popular piece featuring the cats helping with the logs in the garden. The old wheelbarrow was a favourite place for Peter and his brother to hide. They used to turn it upside down and creep underneath to watch the rest of the family try to find them.

Code: HS014
Issued: late 1990
Retired: 1994
Issue Price: £30

THE POTTING SHED

The marking on this piece says 'P Fagan © 86'. The date refers to when Peter actually completed his original sculpture and not to the time of release (1987).

Code: HS015
Issued: early 1987
Retired: 1992
Issue Price: £20

THE OUTSIDE PRIVY

In the 'olden days' when plumbing was primitive and not everyone could afford those more modern conveniences, Peter's Granny was proud of the little brick-built shed at the bottom of the garden! There were lots of names for it from 'The North Pole' to 'The Palace'. Peter often visited his Granny and therefore used to have to trudge down the garden at all hours to 'pay a visit'! He often found it rather chilly on a winter's evening and a long walk back up the dark garden. It became the winter quarters for all kinds of miniature wildlife and once Peter's Granny was convinced there was a mouse 'in residence!' The cats were called in to find the culprit, but they just spent the time chasing each other off the roof! It was Peter's father's job to empty the bucket and very soon a trail of small mounds began to creep up the garden where he buried the contents. Peter remembers with amusement the fact that they moved house before the mounds reached the back door!

The roof, complete with inquisitive cat and brick, is cast separately from the rest of the piece: to extract such a design intact from a single block mould would be impractical.

Code: HS016
Issued: 1988
Issue Price: £22

THE COAL HOLE

Code: HS017
Issued: 1988
Retired: 1992
Issue Price: £22

The Coal Hole demonstrates very well the detail in which Peter Fagan sculpts his pieces. He modelled the walls just as a real wall would be built — brick by brick.

Code: HS021/ XHS021
Issued: 1991
Retired: Spring 1995
Issue Price: £30

Code: HS108
Issued: Mar 1992
Issue Price: £30

THE WARDROBE ▶

The Wardrobe has the rosette marking which features on numerous pieces sculpted in 1992. There is also a sign on the back which reads: 'Made in Great Brit(ain) by Fagan Cabinet Makers'!

ON THE FENCE ▲

Originally released as XHS021 as one of the 1991 Christmas pieces (see advertisement in Collectors Club magazine no.16 — Autumn '91), On the Fence then side slipped into the regular Home Sweet Home collection with the slightly modified code number HS021.

THE SOFA

The Sofa went through a number of permutations before its release in 1992. Originally Peter sculpted a second cat sitting on top of the sofa back, but it proved too difficult in production as the cat tended to rip the moulds. So the cat was replaced by a mouse! Unfortunately the same problem recurred, and the rodent, too, had to go. The piece that was eventually released has neither. Greenware versions of the originals (with cat and mouse) are still in existence in the Colour Box archives, and one of them is marked 'P Fagan 1989'; so clearly these changes took quite a while.

Master painter Terry Fairbairn remembers trying all kinds of colours for the sofa itself until eventually settling on the pink flower pattern.

Code: HS109
Issued: Mar 1992
Issue Price: £20

KITCHEN RANGE

Code: HS110
Issued: 1984
Retired: Spring 1995
Issue Price: £14

Peter's family came from Galway in Ireland and he has many warm and happy memories of his grandmother's house. She was a small, energetic lady with sparkling blue eyes. Her generous nature was famous throughout the area and although the family was very poor, she was always ready to share all she had. In the back kitchen there was a peat fire and a large black pot in which she cooked stews and soups. The west coast of Ireland is cold in winter and Peter remembers the early days when the house was cosy and warm with the rich smell of burning peat and the appetising aroma of Granny's famous Irish Stews (which is still Peter's favourite dinner!). When the family moved to Essex, Granny decided to move too and came to live in a little house close to Peter's family. Obviously she couldn't bring the peat fire, so she had a wonderful range put into the back kitchen. She still cooked delicious soups and Peter's favourite Irish Stews. The cooking pot was the same and the warmth and comfort of the crackling glow. Peter's Granny never wanted an electric stove. She always said she liked 'the living flame' as it made her feel at home and somehow Peter always thought she was right.

Colour variations exist to this piece: early versions have a light brown clock, on later versions it is dark brown. The pots and pans also may vary in colour. Interestingly, the marking on the back of Kitchen Range tells more precisely than usual when it was sculpted: 'Peter Fagan April '84.'   On the mantlepiece is a ginger Striped Cat (H1).

TOILET

Code: HS111
Issued: 1986
Issue Price: £14

The piece is signed and dated: P Fagan © 86 and, like Fireplace (HS310), has the unusual feature of Black Cat (H10) painted brown.

WASHBASIN

The cat here is a ginger Striped Cat (H1).

Code: HS112
Issued: 1986
Retired: 1989
Issue Price: £14

THE BREAKFAST TABLE

The tablecloth is pink on early pieces but was later changed to green. At the same time Grey Cat (H31) was added to the table top.

Code: HS113
Issued: early 1987
Retired: 1989
Issue Price: £14

WASH TUB

Code: HS114
Issued: early 1987
Retired: 1989
Issue Price: £14

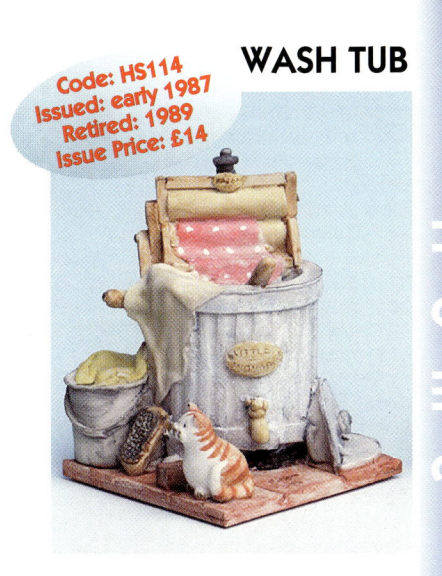

TALLBOY

Code: HS117
Issued: 1989
Retired: 1992
Issue Price: £15

In the corner of Peter's grandmother's house stood a corner cupboard which was always referred to as The Tall Boy! It wasn't a tallboy really but it was always known as that. There was quite a calamity on the day that it was moved from her home to the house in Essex where Peter lived as a boy. It tipped and fell in the removal van and the back of the cupboard was damaged. Peter's father mended it but it was never quite the same, so it was put in the corner of the hall where it was frequented by cats who loved to play hide and seek on the shelves. They broke a plate on one occasion and knowing they'd be in trouble they hid for several hours, one of them on top of the cupboard itself! Sadly the real tallboy no longer exists as it became so tatty that it was eventually moved to the shed and then chopped up and later burnt, but Peter still remembers it well, another memory of his childhood.

The two cats on the piece are a grey Striped Cat (H1) and Frightened Cat (H37). Tallboy is not marked with a signature or date.

HIGH CHAIR

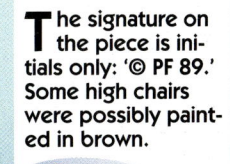

The signature on the piece is initials only: '© PF 89.' Some high chairs were possibly painted in brown.

Code: HS116
Issued: 1989
Retired: 1991
Issue Price: £11

Home Sweet Home

23

THE SECRETARY

Code: HS118
Issued: early 1990
Retired: 1994
Issue Price: £19

The old desk belongs to Peter's father-in-law and has been in the family for years. Frances remembers playing hide-and-seek when she was little, using the knee hole of the desk as her best place to hide. Her pet cat Nibbs used to help her hide under the desk, although the inspiration for this particular piece came from one of Peter's cats who insisted on tapping his pen when he was writing.
On the first 500 pieces the desk was painted with a brown wash; the colour was then changed to cream.

Code: HS119
Issued: late 1990
Retired: 1992
Issue Price: £12

BRING ON THE CLOWNS

A favourite toy and a very happy miniature in which we see a curious cat and a very jolly little toy clown. Peter used Lucy's nightie case to help model this one. At Colour Box the piece was called 'Andy Pandy' before acquiring its final name.

◀ CHIMNEY SWEEP

Code: HS120
Issued: Sept 1993
Issue Price: £20

BEDSTEAD ▼

This marvellous old-fashioned bed is very like the one Peter had as a child. The cat is Ultimate, one of the Fagan family's cats, who wakes Peter up every morning by scratching at the bedroom door. She usually waits at the end of the bed until she can see that Peter is awake and then creeps quietly up towards him, sitting very near him and tapping him with her paw until he takes notice of her. She will always join in the toast if there is any available, and more often than not she will sit on top of the newspaper rather than let it fall down by the side of the bed, as on the piece.

Code: HS210
Issued: 1984
Issue Price: £10

Originally introduced as Bedstead Bliss — the name was changed to Bedstead in 1986. Although the piece has remained consistent over more than ten years of production, some painting variations do exist: 1) The bedspread is brick red on early pieces and was changed to pink; 2) The socks hanging over the end of the bed can be cream (early) or pink; 3) The books on the floor are green (early) or blue (Peter's signature and the date can be found on book cover); 4) The wood is dark with a shading effect (early) or lighter and one colour only. On the bed sits Sleeping Cat (H28).

WELSH DRESSER

Code: HS211
Issued: 1983
Retired: Spring 1995
Issue Price: £10

More recently, Big Black Cat (H42) sits contentedly on the piece, but in earlier times it was a ginger Striped Cat (H1). Painting changes have also been made to a number of details, such as the plates, jug and T-towel.

KITCHEN SINK CAT

Code: HS212
Issued: 1983
Retired: 1990
Issue Price: £10

Originally released as Old Stone Sink, the name was changed to Kitchen Sink Cat in 1985. It is sometimes referred to in Colour Box literature as just Kitchen Sink. This piece features Black Cat (H10).

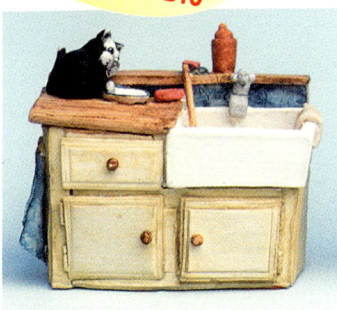

WASHSTAND ▼

The piece does not have a signature or a date.

Code: HS213
Issued: 1989
Retired: 1992
Issue Price: £11

PIANO POPS

Code: HS213
Issued: 1986
Issue Price: £12

The piano belonged to Peter's grandmother and he remembers well the days when she would sit down and play for the children. He also recalls that his grandmother's cat, whose name was Bungle, rarely stayed in the room when the singing began. He would run out and sit on the front doormat howling to go out. Peter claims it was his way of joining in the singing!

The cats sitting on the piano may seem familiar; they are none other than Cats' Chorus (HS412). Ever since its launch in 1986, Piano Pops has remained one of Colour Box's best-selling pieces.

Home Sweet Home

25

BATH TUB ▶

Code: HS214
Issued: early 1987
Retired: 1989
Issue Price: £12

Peter originally sculpted the bath back in 1984 as one of the Mutts Collection (without a cat inside) and called it Bath Tub Terror (the terror being the Mutts' fear of bathtime!). He then introduced the piece into the Home Sweet Home range as Bath Tub in 1987, complete with Grey Cat (H31) in the bath. It was retired two years later but reappeared yet again (by popular demand) in 1991 as Bath (HS538), with alterations: the outside of the bath changed from brown to white, a blue towel changed to pink and a brown book became a green book. The cat inside the bath also changed from H31 to Begging Cat (H38).

GAS STOVE

Code: HS215
Issued: 1986
Retired: 1989
Issue Price: £12

There are two versions of this piece: Mould 1 has a slightly thicker base and has a second cat — Frightened Cat (H37) — sitting on the top of the stove. Mould 2 has a thinner base and just one cat — Plain Cat (H2) — sitting on the tiled floor.

SCHOOL DAYS ▼

Code: HS216
Issued: late 1987
Retired: 1989
Issue Price: £12

POST BOX ▼

Code: HS217
Issued: late 1991
Issue Price: £14.50

CADDY CAT

Code: HS218
Issued: July 1995
Issue Price: £16.50 (price not confirmed)
(No picture available prior to publication.)

OLD FIREPLACE ▶

Code: HS310
Issued: 1983
Issue Price: £7

The name was abbreviated to just Fireplace in 1985. The cats on this piece are painted in unusual colours: Plain Cat (H2), on the mantlepiece, is light brown on early and ginger striped on later pieces; Black Cat (H10), by the hearth, is brown striped.

DAYBREAK

Code: HS311
Issued: late 1987
Retired: 1991
Issue Price: £7

The original version — Mould 1 — of Daybreak is marginally taller and the base bigger; on Mould 2 the curtain rail is thinner and the catch on the window smaller. Early pieces are painted with yellow curtains and have a dark striped cat; later pieces have pink curtains and a ginger striped cat. There are also painting changes to the butterfly in the window and the plant on the window ledge.

GANG'S CHAIR ▶

Code: HS312
Issued: 1983
Issue Price: £7

Gang's Chair, Solo's Chair and Vacant Chair are three variations of the same sculpture — the difference being the number of cats Peter added to them. In all three versions, pieces were painted in a choice of either 1) blue with a white flower pattern and white cushion centre or 2) pink with a white flower pattern. Code numbers were prefixed by 'U' for blue (HS312U) or 'K' for pink (e.g. HS312K). The blue version was issued slightly before the pink. For Gang's Chair the colour choice was changed in 1991 to either purple or grey (Vacant Chair and Solo's Chair had retired by then). Of the two, purple proved the more popular and grey was discontinued in 1993. Purple is now the only colour currently available in 1995. The 'Gang' consists of three Hopscotch cats; Striped Cat (H1), Plain Cat (H2) and Sleeping Cat (H28). (SEE ALSO Solo's Chair [HS410] and Vacant Chair [HS510].)

SIDEBOARD

Code: HS313
Issued: 1984
Retired: 1992
Issue Price: £7

Peter's mother still has the clock on the sideboard, although it's now on the mantlepiece in her living room. Peter remembers it well from childhood days.
This is one of the first pieces Peter ever made for the Colour Box collections and features Plain Cat (H2). On early pieces the sideboard is a light brown colour, but this was later changed to a pine colour. Sideboard has no date marking or signature and is very similar to the base of Welsh Dresser (HS211).

LIBRARIAN

Code: HS314
Issued: 1986
Issue Price: £8

TOOL BOX

Peter's grandfather used to own the box which is made of strong timber and weighs an incredible amount. One character always had a use for the toolbox and he can be seen mischievously looking out from amongst the debris of nails and chisels. Frances Fagan: "The cat always got into the box whenever Peter started to work on anything and, being very soft, Peter never threw him out, so hardly any jobs got finished. The toolbox has now been banished to the shed, but somehow I'm sure the cats will find it out again."

Peter sculpted this piece towards the end of 1986 ready for release in early 1987, hence the marking '© P Fagan 86.' Early pieces have a white cat with black spots; later ones have a grey striped cat.

Code: HS316
Issued: early 1987
Retired: 1992
Issue Price: £9

GRAMOPHONE ▶

The gramophone in question belonged to Frances and her brothers when they were little and was given to Peter because he loves the quality of sound that old 78s make (he's never had much patience with modern music centres!).

As with Tool Box, Gramophone is marked '86', the date it was sculpted, rather than '87' when it was released.

CLOCK-WATCHER

This piece is signed on the base — 'P Fagan' — but is not dated.

Code: HS315
Issued: 1984
Retired: Spring 1995
Issue Price: £7

GOURMET CAT ▼

Unusually, this piece is marked with the actual name 'GOURMET CAT' (in front of the rolling pin) as well the conventional date and signature.

Code: HS318
Issued: late 1987
Retired: 1991
Issue Price: £8

Code: HS317
Issued: early 1987
Retired: 1994
Issue Price: £9

28

FESTIVE FUN

Festive Fun and Yuletide (XHS014) share some similar sculptural detail, namely the two stockings and the gift-wrapped parcel. A framed picture of a cat, also to be seen on Yuletide, was intended as part of Festive Fun, leaning against the front of the piece. (A photograph of this version can be seen in the 1988 Home Sweet Home brochure.) However, this caused production problems and the picture was not included on the released model. Festive Fun's code number (HS319) was reused in 1994 for Bright & Early.

Code: HS319
Issued: late 1987
Retired: 1989
Issue Price: £8

BRIGHT & EARLY

Bright & Early shares the same code number (HS319) as Festive Fun.

Code: HS319
Issued: Mar 1994
Issue Price: £13

EASTER BONNET ▼

Code: HS320
Issued: 1988
Retired: 1992
Issue Price: £5

DRESSING UP

Code: HS321
Issued: 1988
Retired: 1992
Issue Price: £6.50

THE EPICURE

Code: HS322
Issued: 1988
Retired: 1994
Issue Price: £6.50

BIRD SANCTUARY

Code: HS323
Issued: Jul 1994
Issue Price: £13

TAKE THE BISCUIT

Code: HS333
Issued: early 1990
Retired: 1993
Issue Price: £10

Code: HS334
Issued: Mar 1992
Retired: 1994
Issue Price: £12

DRINKS ALL ROUND

Originally issued as Christmas Tipple (XHS022), the name was changed so the piece would have appeal not just at Christmas but all year round.

SOLO'S CHAIR ▼

Solo's Chair features Sleeping Cat (H28) and was available for a very short time in brown, then changed to a choice of either blue or (a little later) pink. SEE ALSO Gang's Chair (HS312) and in particular Vacant Chair (HS510) for details of a mould variation.

Code: HS410
Issued: 1983
Retired: 1990
Issue Price: £6

THE LISTENER

There is a signature on the side of this piece but no date. Note the inscription on the rear: MOG RADIO!

Code: HS411
Issued: 1984
Retired: 1991
Issue Price: £5

CAT'S CHORUS ▼

Have you ever been tempted to throw open the window in the early hours of the morning and throw a slipper at the cat next door who seems to be holding a concert on the back wall? Well, Peter Fagan has. No matter how much he likes his own and his neighbours' cats he can't stand the noise if they start to practise opera at the end of the garden. It always seemed to be the same cats and no matter how accurate Peter's throw, they never learnt and always came back!

Cat's Chorus has been around for more than a decade and during that time it has remained unchanged. The 'chorus' bears an uncanny resemblance to the one performing on Piano Pops (HS213)!

Code: HS412
Issued: 1984
Issue Price: £5

WASHDAY

Colour variations exist to this piece. Earlier versions have a white cloth inside the tub, whilst on later pieces it is salmon with white spots. The towel hanging over the edge also changed, from blue to green. There is also a change to the size of the piece: Mould 1 has a thinner base, bigger soap, bigger cat and bigger tub than Mould 2.

Code: HS413
Issued: 1986
Retired: 1991
Issue Price: £5

BIRD TABLE

Code: HS414
Issued: 1986
Retired: 1990
Issue Price: £5

BARREL

A dark brown striped cat is found on some examples of Barrel — an unusual colour seen perhaps on only one other piece in the collection, the original version of Daybreak (HS311).

Code: HS415
Issued: 1986
Retired: 1989
Issue Price: £5

GLADSTONE BAG ▶

Peter Fagan sculpted Gladstone Bag during the end of the year prior to its release, hence the marking: 'P Fagan © 86.'

Code: HS416
Issued: early 1987
Retired: Spring 1995
Issue Price: £8

Home Sweet Home

A STITCH IN TIME

Code: HS417
Issued: early 1987
Retired: 1992
Issue Price: £5

WATERING CAN

The piece is marked with the date of sculpting: 'P Fagan © 86.' Some colour variations exist: early pieces have a green watering can whilst on later models the can is cream. The colours of the cloths also vary. Some unusual cat colours also exist on this piece — striped fawn.

Code: HS418
Issued: early 1987
Retired: 1990
Issue Price: £5

BIRTHDAY TREAT

Code: HS420
Issued: late 1987
Retired: Spring 1995
Issue Price: £10

TRAVELLER

Early versions of Traveller have a brown trunk; this was later changed to white. At the same time, the towel (or cloth) hanging out of the trunk changed from red to blue. The colour of other detail may also vary. The piece is marked 'P Fagan © 86.'

Code: HS419
Issued: early 1987
Retired: 1994
Issue Price: £10

SUPPERTIME

Code: HS422
Issued: early 1990
Retired: 1993
Issue Price: £8

TUTTI FRUTTI

Code: HS423
Issued: 1988
Retired: Spring 1995
Issue Price: £8

LICK AND PROMISE

Code: HS424
Issued: late 1990
Retired: 1994
Issue Price: £8

The old fashioned way of having a wash and brush up! Here we see the old pitcher and bowl that Grannie would have used before modern plumbing changed everyone's morning wash routines!

AFTERNOON STROLL

Code: HS425
Issued: late 1991
Issue Price: £9

It's time for a walk for one naughty little kitten who managed to climb into the doll's pram for a quiet nap. Little did this mischief know that he was about to be taken for a stroll in the park with the dolly's bottle made up in case he got hungry. He looks warm and comfortable and not particularly disturbed by the exercise and maybe he might even make a habit of it! This piece is modelled on Lucy Fagan's pram. A colourway with a blue pram, pale green blanket and green/white striped ball was produced in November 1993 for Lynn's Cards and Gifts, Woking. In the USA this piece is part of the Pennywhistle Lane collection.

ALI-BABA

Code: HS426
Issued: Mar 1992
Issue Price: £10

EARLY BLOOMERS

Code: HS427
Issued: Mar 1992
Issue Price: £10

THE GROUNDSMAN

Code: HS434
Issued: Jun 1992
Retired: Spring 1995
Issue Price: £10

Home Sweet Home

BIN STEALING

Code: HS435
Issued: Jun 1992
Issue Price: £10

THE LAST DROP

Code: HS436
Issued: Jun 1992
Issue Price: £10

BUILDERS' MATE ▶

Code: HS437
Issued: Mar 1993
Issue Price: £10

This piece was sculpted to raise money for the Cats Protection League, a national charity which looks after homeless cats. All net profits from the sale of the piece from the date of issue until 31st December 1993 were donated to CPL. The cat on the piece is based on 'Leroy' (now deceased) from the Mabel Jenkins Shelter in Birmingham who was selected by Collectors Club members in a competition.

▼ HIGH TIME

Code: HS439
Issued: Feb 1995
Issue Price: £11.25

WINTER SPORT

Code: HS438
Issued: Jul 1994
Issue Price: £11

THE THOROUGHBRED

Code: HS440
Issued: July 1995
Issue Price: £11.25
(No picture available prior to publication.)

34

VACANT CHAIR ▶

Code: HS510
Issued: 1983
Retired: 1989
Issue Price: £5

When Vacant Chair was first issued in brown, the flower pattern was recessed into the chair (Mould 1) and not painted. It looked rather drab and Peter soon changed the colour to blue and (a little later) pink, with the flowers highlighted in other colours. However, it proved very difficult for painters to follow accurately the recessed lines and so the 'greenware' was altered, smoothing the patterns over (Mould 2). Painters could then add the flowers 'freehand', and have done so ever since. The same mould variation applies to Solo's Chair but (probably) not to Gang's Chair, which was issued later. Brown models are now very rare and in great demand amongst serious collectors. See also Solo's Chair (HS410) and Gang's Chair (HS312) for more information.

LAUNDRY LAYABOUT ▼

There are two painted versions of Laundry Layabout: early pieces have a black and white cat and a green cloth peg bag; later ones have a grey striped cat and a pink peg bag.

Code: HS512
Issued: 1986
Retired: 1993
Issue Price: £8

CATS' CRADLE

Code: HS511
Issued: 1986
Retired: 1993
Issue Price: £6

Originally the cradle was painted brown and the cat was fawn with blue blanket and pillow edging. In 1988 the cradle was changed to white, and at the same time a choice of pink or blue for the blanket, pillow and knobs on cradle corners was made available. (N.B. A brown cradle with pink blanket should not exist, but who knows . . .) Some pieces are marked 'P Fagan' whilst others include the copyright symbol and date (© 84).

TRASH CAN CAT

Code: HS514
Issued: 1983
Retired: 1991
Issue Price: £5

Despite its code number, Trash Can Cat was in fact the first Colour Box sculpture Peter made. "I painted one of my bronze figurines of a cat to give it some humour, " he explains, "and it sold like wildfire. So I though of developing the theme and putting the same cat into different situations. The idea of him scavenging on top of an old dustbin came to me first." The cat balancing precariously on the piece is Plain Cat (H2).

35

LAMP

Code: HS516
Issued: early 1987
Retired: 1989
Issue Price: £5

The base of the lamp is not unlike the bronze lamp stands that Peter used to make in the 1970s in the pre-Colour Box days. Two versions are known to exist: Mould 1 has a slightly thicker base, a black cat, and a taller lamp with the central bulbous part painted blue; Mould 2 has a thinner base, a fawn cat, a shorter lamp with the central part painted green.

LUNCH BOX

Code: HS517
Issued: early 1987
Retired: 1992
Issue Price: £5

Marking reads: '© 86 P Fagan.'

PACKING CAT ▼

Code: HS518
Issued: early 1987
Retired: 1992
Issue Price: £5

Early pieces have a white cat with black patches, the cloth overhanging the edge of the box is light blue with dark blue polka dots, and the cloth inside the box is yellow. Later (more common) pieces have a black cat with a white face, a blue cloth overhanging the box edge and a pink cloth inside. The piece is marked with the year it was sculpted: '© 86 P Fagan.' This was the year Peter and Frances Fagan moved to their cottage in West Wellow, Hampshire, and the words 'West Wellow' can be seen on the side of the packing case!

FIRESIDE FRIEND ▼

Code: HS519
Issued: late 1987
Retired: 1992
Issue Price: £5

THE ARTIST

Code: HS520
Issued: early 1990
Retired: 1992
Issue Price: £5

TAKEAWAY

Code: HS521
Issued: early 1990
Issue Price: £5

HOME COOKING

Code: HS522
Issued: early 1990
Retired: 1991
Issue Price: £5

INCONVENIENCE ▼

A special Inconvenience colourway was created for a promotion at 'Just Right' (or 'I'r Dim', as it is in Welsh) in Denbigh to celebrate the shop's tenth anniversary in 1993. The piece had 'I'r Dim' painted on the side instead of the usual 'His' and a gold rim. A colourway of Sullivan (Teddies Collection) was also created for the same event. Inconvenience and Chambermaid (HS525) are closely related pieces!

Code: HS524
Issued: 1991
Retired: Spring 1995
Issue Price: £4.50

GONE FISHING

Code: HS523
Issued: early 1990
Retired: 1994
Issue Price: £7

CHAMBERMAID

Code: HS525
Issued: late 1991
Retired: 1994
Issue Price: £5

COMFY CAT ▼

Code: HS526
Issued: late 1991
Retired: 1994
Issue Price: £5

37

CENTRE FOLD

Code: HS527
Issued: 1991
Issue Price: £5

SIXPENNY CORNET

Code: HS528
Issued: late 1991
Retired: 1994
Issue Price: £5

PRIMA BALLERINA

Code: HS529
Issued: 1991
Issue Price: £5

FISH SUPPER

Code: HS530
Issued: Feb 1991
Retired: 1993
Issue Price: £8

FIRST FORMER ▼

1991 was Lucy Fagan's first year at 'proper' school — the inspiration for this piece.

Code: HS531
Issued: Feb 1991
Retired: 1993
Issue Price: £8

FOOTBALL CRAZY ▼

A number of colourways have been produced, including two 'one-offs' in Hearts and Hibs colours — see list in Other Items.

Code: HS532
Issued: Feb 1991
Retired: 1993
Issue Price: £8

RIGHT ON TIME

Code: HS533
Issued: 1991
Retired: Spring 1995
Issue Price: £8

JUST GOOD FRIENDS

A variation exists to the bow around the grey cat's neck. Originally (Mould 1) a bow was just painted on (and occasionally not!); then Peter altered the 'master' by sculpting a bow onto the cat (Mould 2). The change was made so that homepainters would have something more precise to follow. See also picture on page 14.

Code: HS534
Issued: 1991
Issue Price: £8

KISS IT BETTER ▶

Code: HS535
Issued: Feb 1991
Retired: 1994
Issue Price: £8

There are four paint variations to the cross on this piece. In the autumn of 1991 the International Red Cross contacted Colour Box to inform them that the use of the red cross on Kiss It Better was in breach of the Geneva Convention! So Colour Box decided to change the cross to green. However, pieces in shops with the red cross (Version 1) were left unchanged, and pieces in production which had already been given a red cross were overpainted with a dark green gloss paint (it proved impossible to remove the red paint). This gave the effect of a deep green cross with feint red edges (Version 2). New, unpainted pieces, were originally given several coats of green to create a gloss effect (Version 3), but by the end of 1992 just one coat had become standard to give a paler matt green effect (Version 4). Of these four versions, the first two are rare.

Similarly the red cross on First Aid Post in the Teddy Bear Collection and Tender Care from the Early Days Range were also changed to green.

BEACH BOY

Code: HS536
Issued: Feb 1991
Retired: 1994
Issue Price: £8

Home Sweet Home

39

THE DECORATOR

Originally the paint in the tin was red; this was later changed to green.

Code: HS537
Issued: Feb 1991
Retired: 1994
Issue Price: £8

BATH

Originally issued in 1987 as Bath Tub (HS214) with the outside painted brown. This was changed to white for reissue with the shorter name. Early pieces do not have a cat sitting in the bath and Begging Cat (H38) was added later. All these versions descend from an even earlier piece in the Mutts Collection — Bath Tub Terror.

Code: HS538
Issued: 1991
Issue Price: £16.50

THE BUSKER

A musical cat with large ambitions — that squeeze box looks quite a challenge.

Code: HS539
Issued: late 1991
Retired: Spring 1995
Issue Price: £8

MOSES BASKET (Blue)

Code: HS 540
Issued: Mar 1992
Issue Price: £8

MOSES BASKET (Pink)

Code: HS541
Issued: Mar 1992
Issue Price: £8

NICE 'N' COSY

Code: HS542
Issued: Mar 1992
Issue Price: £8

THE CORRESPONDENT

Does your cat like to help? Peter Fagan's cats are all very helpful, especially when he's busy at his desk. Peter is not a very good correspondent and usually waits till the very last moment to answer letters so he takes even longer when the cat decides to join him on the desk and help lick the envelopes. She always sits in the middle of everything and loves the sound of the paper rustling. It's a good job she's not quite tall enough to reach the letter box!

In the USA a colourway version of this piece called Christmas Correspondent is included in the Pennywhistle Lane collection (the letters in the rack are changed to Christmas cards).

Code: HS543
Issued: Jun 1992
Retired: Spring 1995
Issue Price: £8

THE DAILY GRIND

KNIT ONE PURL ONE

Code: HS544
Issued: Jun 1992
Retired: 1994
Issue Price: £8

Code: HS545
Issued: Mar 1993
Issue Price: £8

TEACHER'S PET

Code: HS546
Issued: Sept 1993
Issue Price: £78

CAT CALL

Code: HS547
Issued: Sept 1993
Issue Price: £8

Home Sweet Home

41

BE MY VALENTINE

Code: HS548
Issued: Sept 1993
Issue Price: £8

GIFT WRAP CAT

Code: HS549
Issued: Jul 1994
Issue Price: £8.50

FIRE ENGINE

Code: HS550
Issued: Jul 1994
Issue Price: £8.50

WATCH THE BIRDIE

Code: HS551
Issued: Feb 1995
Issue Price: £8.75

BOWLED OVER

Code: HS552
Issued: Feb 1995
Issue Price: £8.75

SHIPMATE

Code: HS553
Issued: Feb 1995
Issue Price: £8.75

THE EXECUTIVE

Code: HS554
Issued: Feb 1995
Issue Price: £8.75

THE OPPORTUNIST

Such is Peter Fagan's attention to detail that he first sculpted the jug intact, and then broke it into pieces to ensure all the segments matched.

Code: HS609
Issued: 1988
Retired: 1993
Issue Price: £5

BOOKWORM ▼

Bookworm is one of the most popular pieces in the Home Sweet Home range. A colourway, with a grey striped cat instead of the usual pale ginger striped, and pink and blue books with gold corners, was produced in June 1994 for 'Cameo House', Chesham. A colourway is also marketed in the USA as part of the Pennywhistle Lane collection.

Code: HS610
Issued: 1984
Issue Price: £4

CAT BASKET ▼

On early (rare) models the basket was painted cream; this was changed to brown on more recent pieces. The cat in the basket is Sleeping Cat (H28). A colourway is being launched in the USA in 1995 as part of the Pennywhistle Lane collection.

Code: HS611
Issued: 1983
Retired: 1992
Issue Price: £4

KETTLE

Code: HS612
Issued: 1986
Retired: Spring 1995
Issue Price: £5

Home Sweet Home

COAL SKUTTLE

In some Colour Box literature this piece is also referred to as Coal Skuttle Cat. The cat (cast separately) is Black Cat (H10) but painted brown.

Code: HS613
Issued: 1983
Retired: 1990
Issue Price: £4

FLAT CAP ▼

There are two clearly defined painting variations to this piece: 1) Early versions have a brown cap with red lines; 2) On later versions the cap is cream with brown lines. The piece is marked: 'P Fagan © 86.'

Code: HS615
Issued: late 1987
Retired: 1993
Issue Price: £4

WEE WILLIE WINKIE ▼

Code: HS617
Issued: 1988
Retired: 1992
Issue Price: £5

BOOT

Boot was painted in black or brown, and with cats varying from ginger to grey.

Code: HS614
Issued: 1988
Retired: 1992
Issue Price: £5

FIRESIDE COMFORT

About 300 of a special colourway with a 'magenta' slipper were produced for a promotion at Church's, a store in Northampton, in September 1992. Although issued in 1988, some labels read '1987'.

Code: HS616
Issued: 1988
Retired: 1993
Issue Price: £5

THE TROMBONIST

Code: HS618
Issued: 1989
Retired: 1993
Issue Price: £8

Frances Fagan: *"When Paul, my eldest was only seven, he announced a surprising interest in learning the trombone. It was a shock to all of us as we might have expected the recorder or even the guitar, but the trombone was certainly different! We believe it came from a visit to the Edinburgh Tattoo the year before when the magnificent marching and military precision of the bandsmen impressed him greatly. Perhaps it was connected to the fact that the trombonists always seemed to lead the band since if they were placed anywhere else there would be a serious danger of causing injury to the instrumentalists going ahead! Well, whatever the reason, we were lent a magnificent silver trombone and Paul began his lessons. The effect on the cats was quite unbelievable! At first they were fascinated by the extraordinary rude noises that issued forth, but after some considerable practise the noises grew louder and became quite alarming to both cats (we didn't have Cinders at this time). Trombone lessons became times to be dreaded by the feline members of the family, when one of the cats used to take to hiding under the bed. Inevitably, as time went by, they became accustomed to it and even a little bold as they investigated the case. Perhaps it was the velvet lining that was so attractive to them. Paul never got good enough at it to lead the military tattoo, so when it was dropped for more passive activities the cats were very relieved!"*

TOP HAT CAT ▶

Code: HS619
Issued: 1989
Retired: 1990
Issue Price: £5

Top hat Cat created major production problems as the rim of the hat tended to break off during extraction from the mould — hence the brief production run. This piece is now highly collectable. The code number of Top Hat Cat (HS619) was later reused for One for the Pot.

ONE FOR THE POT ▼

One for the Pot has the same code number as Top Hat Cat.

Code: HS619
Issued: Mar 1992
Retired: Spring 1995
Issue Price: £5

PIANO STOOL ▶

Code: HS620
Issued: 1989
Retired: 1991
Issue Price: £5

When Piano Stool retired in 1991, the code number HS620 was reallocated to Stoke It Up the following year.

STOKE IT UP

Has same code number as Piano Stool.

Code: HS620
Issued: Mar 1992
Issue Price: £5

FLOWER POWER ▼

Peter Fagan: "At home, we have some large earthenware flower pots which we put outside our front porch. Every year the flower pots lie in the sun with little trailing plants growing over the edges and we also put annuals in them to give a bit of colour. The cats totally ignore the pots for all but one week in the year, the week when we have just planted up the pots. Then we find the cats curled up on top of the new plants and without fail we have to replant the pots because the seedlings have been flattened by a heavy feline weight. Why they choose that particular time to flatten the plants is a mystery to me, I suppose it's just part of the way cats like to be in the middle of everything. But it is coming up to that time of year again, so remembering this I modelled Flower Power for you with a very smug cat squashing my flowers."

When it was retired Flower Power's code number was reallocated to Pastry Cook.

Code: HS621
Issued: 1989
Retired: 1992
Issue Price: £5

PASTRY COOK

Has the same code number as Flower Power.

Code: HS621
Issued: Jun 1992
Retired: Feb 1995
Issue Price: £5

DUSTPAN PUSS ▶

Dustpan Puss retired in 1991 and the following year its code number (HS622) was reassigned to Flat Cat.

Code: HS622
Issued: 1989
Retired: 1991
Issue Price: £5

46

FLAT CAT

Code: HS622
Issued: Jun 1992
Retired: 1994
Issue Price: £5

The code number HS622 orginally belonged to Dustpan Puss. Shortly after release, the stripes on the cat were simplified for ease of painting.

EXTRA PINT

Code: HS624
Issued: Mar 1992
Issue Price: £2

KATY'S BASKET ▼

The Katy in question is Katy Read, winner of a junior design competition held by the Colour Box Collectors Club in 1988. The prize was to have her drawing transformed into a model by Peter Fagan, and Katy's Basket is an accurate interpretation of Katy's drawing (which was reproduced in issue 4 of the Club newsletter).

Code: HS623
Issued: 1989
Retired: 1992
Issue Price: £8

ROCKING HORSE ▶

Code: HS625
Issued: 1989
Retired: 1992
Issue Price: £15

The rocking horse in question was a present from Father Christmas to Lucy, Peter's youngest daughter.
At the time of its release this was the fastest selling new piece in the Home Sweet Home range. A competition to give the rocking horse a name was launched in the Spring '89 newsletter and won by Clare Dias from Hertfordshire with "Magic" (Lucy chose the winner herself). The signature on this piece is abbreviated to initials: '© PF 89.'

Code: HS626
Issued: October 1992
Issue Price: £4.50

◀ ALL LIT UP

A colourway of All Lit Up with red and green lampshade was produced in October 1993 for Lawleys, Reading.

Home Sweet Home

47

PUSS IN BOOTS ▶

Code: HS627
Issued: Oct 1992
Issue Price: £4.50

A colourway of Puss In Boots with the wellingtons painted dark green all over (including the soles) was produced for Glorious Britain, Gatwick Airport, July 1993. Although the official (and most common) colour of the wellingtons is black, pieces with green boots have also turned up in other stores; they are different from the Glorious Britain colourway in that they retain the beige edging and soles.

Code: HS628
Issued: Jun 1993
Issue Price: £5

DIG & DELVE

Code: HS629
Issued: Mar 1993
Issue Price: £5

EARLY RISER

Code: HS631
Issued: Jun 1993
Issue Price: £45

Code: HS630
Issued: Mar 1993
Issue Price: £5

BIG SPENDER

WATERBED ▲

A colourway with a blue hot water bottle (it's usually red) was produced in November 1993 for Randles, Wellingborough.

KISS ME QUICK

Code: HS632
Issued: Mar 1993
Issue Price: £5

Code: HS633
Issued: Jun 1993
Issue Price: £5

LITTLE SPRINKLER

LITTLE SAVER

Code: HS634
Issued: Sept 1993
Issue Price: £5

Code: HS635
Issued: Sept 1993
Issue Price: £5

WEIGHING IN

STOOL PIGEON ▼

Code: HS637
Issued: Sept 1993
Issue Price: £5

FAST MOVER ▼

Shortly after release, the stripes on the cat were simplified for ease of painting.

Code: HS636
Issued: Sept 1993
Issue Price: £5

Code: HS638
Issued: Sept 1993
Issue Price: £5

THE BRICKIE

PORKER PUSS

Code: HS639
Issued: Mar 1994
Issue Price: £5

Code: HS640
Issued: Feb 1995
Issue Price: £4.99

POP TO THE SHOP

Home Sweet Home

49

LIGHTING UP TIME

Code: HS642
Issued: Feb 1995
Issue Price: £4.99

THE WARDEN

The Warden was very nearly called 'ARP Cat' — both names were considered during pre-production.

Code: HS643
Issued: Feb 1995
Issue Price: £4.99

GREETINGS CAT

Code: HS644
Issued: Feb 1995
Issue Price: £4.99

CONGRATULATIONS CARD CAT

Code: HS645
Issued: July 1995
Issue Price: £4.99 (price not confirmed)
(No picture available prior to publication.)

BEST WISHES CAT

Code: HS646
Issued: July 1995
Issue Price: £4.99 (price not confirmed)
(No picture available prior to publication.)

SINGING CAT

Originally part of the Hopscotch collection (H61).

Code: HS701
Issued: Mar 1992
Retired: Feb 1994
Issue Price: £1.75

50

CAT & WOOL

Originally part of the Hopscotch collection (H62).

Code: HS702
Issued: Mar 1992
Retired: Feb 1994
Issue Price: £1.75

CAT & FISHBONE

Originally part of the Hopscotch collection (H63).

Code: HS703
Issued: Mar 1992
Retired: 1993
Issue Price: £1.75

CAT & TOY MOUSE

Originally part of the Hopscotch collection (H64).

Code: HS704
Issued: Mar 1992
Retired: Spring 1995
Issue Price: £1.75

CAT & BOW

Originally part of the Hopscotch collection (H65).

Code: HS705
Issued: Mar 1992
Retired: 1993
Issue Price: £1.75

CAT & BALL

Originally part of the Hopscotch Collection (H56). A version in solid sterling silver was produced for direct sale to Collectors Club members in 1989. The following year a colourway was included as one of the limited edition Festive Hopscotch pieces.

Code: HS706
Issued: Mar 1992
Retired: 1993
Issue Price: £1.75

Home Sweet Home

BALLOON RACE

Code: HS707
Issued: Mar 1992
Issue Price: £2

GLASS ALLEY CAT

Code: HS708
Issued: Mar 1992
Issue Price: £2

BUTTERFLY CAT

Code: HS709
Issued: Mar 1992
Issue Price: £2

PING PONG PUSS ▼

Code: HS710
Issued: Mar 1992
Issue Price: £2

PETAL PUSS ▼

A colourway of Petal Puss with pink instead of the usual orange petals was created in September 1992 for Cottage Crafts, Sawbridgeworth.

Code: HS711
Issued: Jun 1992
Issue Price: £2

BATHTIME PAL

Code: HS712
Issued: Jun 1992
Issue Price: £2

BAGPUSS

Code: HS713
Issued: Jun 1992
Issue Price: £2

LOTS OF LUCK

Code: HS714
Issued: Sept 1993
Issue Price: £2

A Lots of Luck colourway with a ginger cat was created in September 1993 for Choices, Welwyn. Peter Fagan originally sculpted the horseshoe upside down and hastily resculpted it when informed that an inverted horseshoe actually brings bad luck! The original master before it was corrected (complete with horseshoe upside down) was sold at Christie's in 1993. In the USA Lots of Luck is part of the Pennywhistle Lane collection.

MILKMAID

Code: HS715
Issued: Mar 1993
Issue Price: £2

TASTY MORSEL

Code: HS716
Issued: Jun 1993
Issue Price: £2

Code: HS717
Issued: Mar 1993
Issue Price: £2

MUMMY'S BOY

Code: HS718
Issued: Mar 1993
Issue Price: £2

MUMMY'S GIRL

The only difference between Mummy's Girl and Mummy's Boy (HS718) is the painting of the kitten — black with a pink bow on Mummy's Girl and grey with a blue bow on Mummy's Boy. In the USA Mummy's Girl is part of the Pennywhistle Lane collection.

DOG'S DINNER

Code: HS719
Issued: Mar 1994
Issue Price: £2

BRUSH UP

Code: HS720
Issued: Feb 1995
Issue Price: £1.99

BREADBOARD

Code: HS801
Issued: early 1990
Retired: 1994
Issue Price: £8

MOUSE TRAP

Code: HS802
Issued: early 1990
Retired: 1992
Issue Price: £8

EASTER SURPRISE

Code: HS803
Issued: Mar 1994
Issue Price: £6.50

TOP CAT

Code: HS804
Issued: Mar 1994
Issue Price: £6.50

Code: HS805
Issued: Mar 1994
Issue Price: £6.50

◀ CAT FISH

Home Sweet Home

54

UPSTAIRS, DOWNSTAIRS

Code: HS806
Issued: Mar 1994
Issue Price: £6.50

WAKEY, WAKEY

Code: HS807
Issued: Mar 1994
Issue Price: £6.50

CAT NAPPER ▼

This piece, featuring the Cat Protection League's cat 'sleeper' for keeping kittens snug and warm, was originally sculpted by Peter to raise funds for the CPL and was sold at a Selfridges promotion on 25th Sept 1993 during National Cat Week. Six months later Cat Napper joined the main Home Sweet Home collection, without any painting variation.

Code: HS808
Issued: Mar 1994
Issue Price: £6.50

COSY TOES

Code: HS809
Issued: Jul 1994
Issue Price: £6.50

GRANNY'S KITCHEN

Code: HS900
Issued: Jul 1995
Issue Price: £49.95 (price not confirmed)
(No picture available prior to publication.)

WISHING WELL

Code: HS901
Issued: Jul 1995
Issue Price: £49.95 (price not confirmed)
(No picture available prior to publication.)

HOME SWEET HOME PIECES WITHOUT CODE NUMBERS

Code: None
Issued: 1983
Retired: 1986
Issue Price: £7

HIGH NOON

Peter remembers this and Midnight Cat very well as they were particularly difficult to grind. They stood on a narrow flat base that had to be ground down exactly level or they would fall over. Peter recalls sitting in his studio, an old converted garage, grinding the bases often long into the night, looking out of the little window at the back. High Noon features a ginger Striped Cat (H1). In 1986 Peter Fagan became aware of counterfeit versions of High Noon and so he immediately withdrew the piece and remodelled it, adding curtains, to create Window.

Code: None
Issued: 1983
Retired: 1986
Issue Price: £7

MIDNIGHT CAT

The cat featured on this piece is Reclining Cat (H36).

Code: None
Issued: 1984
Retired: 1987
Issue Price: £10

DOORSTEP DILEMMA

This is the front door of the house where Peter Fagan used to live in Essex when he was a boy. By recent standards it's a fairly simple piece, and Peter says his modelling has become more intricate and detailed since then. Doorstep Dilemma is one of several pieces which were never allocated a 'code number', nor does it have a signature or date marking. A decade later Peter sculpted the back door of the same house (also with a number '7') — see Private Entrance, a 1994/95 Collectors Club piece. Incidentallly, the cat facing the dilemma is a ginger Striped Cat (H1).

Code: None
Issued: 1986
Retired: 1987
Issue Price: £7

WINDOW

Originally the piece was called 'Old Window', but 'old' was soon dropped. Window is an adaptation of High Noon.

Code: None
Issued: 1983
Retired: 1985
Issue Price: £6

THE WALL

A forerunner of Cat's Chorus (HS412) but instead of the 'chorus' there is a single cat and Dove (H26) from the Hopscotch collection.

Personality Pups

Personality Pups first appeared in the Autumn of 1991 and were sculpted in response to many requests from collectors for a range of dogs. In style they are a greatly developed extension of The Mutts, Peter Fagan's collection of five mongrels released in 1984 and retired in 1987. *From pooches needing pedigrees to mongrels needing management, the Personality Pups are guaranteed to win your affection. Papa and Poppet head this endless family of uncles, aunties and cuddlesome cousins with the mischievous puppies up to all their cute canine capers.*
A further ten pieces — the Frou-Frou Collection — were issued a year later in October 1992.

PATRICK

Code: DG001
Issued: Sept 1991
Issue Price: £2
Retired: 1994

PATCH

Code: DG002
Issued: Sept 1991
Issue Price: £2
Retired: 1994

PETULA

Code: DG003
Issued: Sept 1991
Issue Price: £2

PENNY

See Patrick 001

Code: DG004
Issued: Sept 1991
Issue Price: £2
Retired: 1994

PICKLE

Code: DG005
Issued: Sept 1991
Issue Price: £2

POWDER PUFF

Code: DG006
Issued: Sept 1991
Issue Price: £2

PEACEFUL

Code: DG007
Issued: Sept 1991
Issue Price: £2

A colourway of Peaceful with a different coloured bow was produced in September 1992 for Cottage Crafts, Sawbridgeworth.

POLO

Code: DG008
Issued: Sept 1991
Issue Price: £2
Retired: 1993

POGO

Code: DG009
Issued: Sept 1991
Issue Price: £2

PIECRUST

Code: DG010
Issued: Sept 1991
Issue Price: £2

PETER

Code: DG011
Issued: Sept 1991
Issue Price: £2

PEPPERCORN

Code: DG012
Issued: Sept 1991
Issue Price: £2

PRINCE

Code: DG013
Issued: Sept 1991
Issue Price: £2

PANSY

Code: DG014
Issued: Sept 1991
Issue Price: £2

PRECIOUS
Code: DG015
Issued: Sept 1991
Issue Price: £2

PRIMROSE
Code: DG016
Issued: Sept 1991
Issue Price: £2

POM POM
Code: DG017
Issued: Sept 1991
Issue Price: £2

POPPY
Code: DG018
Issued: Sept 1991
Issue Price: £2
Retired: 1993

PING PONG
Code: DG019
Issued: Sept 1991
Issue Price: £2
Retired: 1993

PORKY
Code: DG020
Issued: Sept 1991
Issue Price: £2

PAPA
Code: DG101
Issued: Sept 1991
Issue Price: £3

POPPET
Code: DG102
Issued: Sept 1991
Issue Price: £3

Personality Pups

Personality Pups

THE JUGGLER

Code: DG103
Issued: Sept 1991
Issue Price: £3
Retired: 1993

SHARING A TREAT

Code: DG104
Issued: Sept 1991
Issue Price: £3

ROLY POLY

Code: DG105
Issued: Sept 1991
Issue Price: £3
Retired: 1993

ROUGH AND TUMBLE

Code: DG106
Issued: Sept 1991
Issue Price: £3
Retired: 1994

PLAYTIME

Code: DG107
Issued: Sept 1991
Issue Price: £3
Retired: 1994

DAD'S SLIPPER

Code: DG201
Issued: Sept 1991
Issue Price: £4.50

DROPPED STITCH

Code: DG202
Issued: Sept 1991
Issue Price: £4.50

WRONG SIDE UP

Code: DG203
Issued: Sept 1991
Issue Price: £4.50

TICKLISH PUP

Code: DG204
Issued: Sept 1991
Issue Price: £4.50
Retired: 1994

FATHERLY LOVE

Code: DG205
Issued: Sept 1991
Issue Price: £4.50
Retired: 1994

OOPS A DAISY

Code: DG206
Issued: Sept 1991
Issue Price: £4.50
Retired: 1994

IN THE DOGHOUSE

Code: DG300
Issued: Sept 1991
Issue Price: £11.50

To avoid production problems, the blue tit sitting on the top of the kennel is cast separately and glued into place.

HITCHED UP

Code: DG301
Issued: Sept 1991
Issue Price: £7.75

SEA DOG

Code: DG302
Issued: Sept 1991
Issue Price: £7.75

Living in Essex for most of his boyhood, Peter can remember taking his dog down to the beach for a run most evenings. What his mother never knew was how he used to tie the puppy up to an old bollard near the fishing port entrance whilst he nipped into the fish and chip shop on the corner for six pennyworth of chips and a pennyworth of 'crackling'. He's still very partial to fish and chips, out of the paper of course, whilst walking round any coastal town. He says it tastes better in the open air with the smell of the sea and the gulls to help tidy up! He used to save some of the batter for his puppy who would jump up on top of the bollard in excited expectation when Peter came back to fetch him for the journey home.

Personality Pups

63

FROU-FROU COLLECTION

These pups are French poodlish and have a distinctly mischievous appeal. They look as if they need a good clip but, somehow, they've been able to escape the poodle parlour and dig a hole in the garden instead! None of them could possibly boast a pedigree!

FRIBBLE

Code: DG108
Issued: October 1992
Issue Price: £2.99

FRAZZLE

Code: 109
Issued: October 1992
Issue Price: £2.99

FRENZIE

Code: DG207
Issued: October 1992
Issue Price: £4.99

FRAZER

Code: DG110
Issued: October 1992
Issue Price: £2.99

A colourway of Frazer with a red football with green spots was produced in October 1993 for Lawleys, Reading.

FROLIC

Code: DG208
Issued: October 1992
Issue Price: £4.99

FRIVOLOUS

Code: DG209
Issued: October 1992
Issue Price: £4.99

FRICASSE

The colours were modified on Fricasse, but probably before production began and it is unlikely that any of the original version were released.

Code: DG210
Issued: October 1992
Issue Price: £4.99

Code: DG211
Issued: October 1992
Issue Price: £4.99

FRANKIE

A Frankie colourway with a blue slipper was produced in April 1993 for Lawleys Collectors Weekend.

FREESIA

Code: DG213
Issued: October 1992
Issue Price: £4.99

Code: DG212
Issued: October 1992
Issue Price: £4.99

FREDDIE & FRUITIE

Miniature Collection

This collection of woodland birds and animals was one of the three original Colour Box collections (the other two were Home Sweet Home and Hopscotch) launched in 1983. The first pieces relied heavily upon the earlier cold cast bronze sculptures that Peter Fagan had been creating since 1973. Originally the Miniatures were sold without the wooden plinths which are now standard; they were introduced in Summer 1989 to improve the presentation.

Some code numbers in the collection are duplicated as numbers of retired pieces have been reused (e.g. MC13 = Labrador, Duck and Ducklings; MC16 = Elephant, Puffin; MC18 = Koala, Doe and Fawn). Please note that pieces in this section are listed chronologically by issue date first and code numbers second; therefore reused code numbers will appear out of numerical sequence. A complete set of the Miniature Collection (75 pieces) was auctioned at Christie's in 1993 and fetched £132.

CALF

Code: MC1
Issued: 1983
Retired: 1990
Issue Price: £2

CAT (AND MOUSE)

Code: MC2
Issued: 1983
Retired: 1991
Issue Price: £2

A reworking of a bronze from the pre-Colour Box days. The original name Cat and Mouse was abbreviated to just Cat in 1985 (not to be confused with Cat [H25] from the Hopscotch Collection) and the mouse was removed from the sculpture. The cat was also repainted from black to tabby.

DUCK

Code: MC3
Issued: 1983
Retired: 1992
Issue Price: £2

HEN (AND CHICKS)

Code: MC5
Issued: 1983
Retired: 1989
Issue Price: £2

The piece was originally issued as just Hen.

HEDGEHOGS

Code: MC4
Issued: 1983
Retired: 1992
Issue Price: £2

SEAL (AND PUP)

Code: MC6
Issued: 1983
Retired: 1989
Issue Price: £2

The piece was originally called just Seal. The name changed to Seal and Pup in 1985.

MOUSE (AND TOADSTOOL)

Code: MC7
Issued: 1983
Retired: 1992
Issue Price: £2

Originally launched as Mouse, the name was extended to Mouse and Toadstool in 1986.

OTTER

Code: MC8
Issued: 1983
Retired: 1989
Issue Price: £2

Larger than the other Otter (MC48) launched in 1989.

OWL

Code: MC9
Issued: 1983
Retired: 1992
Issue Price: £2

PIG (AND PIGLETS)

Code: MC10
Issued: 1983
Retired: 1991
Issue Price: £2

The piece was originally issued as Pig. The name was changed to Pig and Piglets in 1985

PONY AND FOAL

Code: MC11
Issued: 1983
Retired: 1991
Issue Price: £2

RABBITS

Code: MC12
Issued: 1983
Retired: 1991
Issue Price: £2

LABRADOR

Code: MC13
Issued: 1983
Retired: 1987
Issue Price: £2

SHEEP AND LAMB

Code: MC14
Issued: 1983
Retired: 1992
Issue Price: £2

SQUIRREL

Code: MC15
Issued: 1983
Retired: 1989
Issue Price: £2

ELEPHANT

Code: MC16
Issued: 1985
Retired: 1987
Issue Price: £2.50

PENGUIN

Code: MC17
Issued: 1985
Retired: 1989
Issue Price: £2.50

Miniature Collection

Miniature Collection

KOALA
Code: MC18
Issued: 1985
Retired: 1989
Issue Price: £2.50

WOODMOUSE
Code: MC19
Issued: 1986
Retired: 1991
Issue Price: £2.50

FOX
Code: MC20
Issued: 1986
Retired: 1989
Issue Price: £2.50

BADGER
Code: MC21
Issued: 1986
Retired: 1989
Issue Price: £2.50

FROG
Code: MC22
Issued: 1986
Retired: 1991
Issue Price: £2.50

MOLE
Code: MC23
Issued: 1986
Retired: 1989
Issue Price: £2.50

SADDLEBACK PIG
Code: MC24
Issued: 1986
Retired: 1991
Issue Price: £2.50

DUCK AND DUCKLINGS
Code: MC13
Issued: 1987
Retired: 1990
Issue Price: £2.50

Duck originally painted white with yellow ducklings, but later changed to a speckled brown duck with beige ducklings.

PUFFIN
Code: MC16
Issued: 1987
Retired: 1989
Issue Price: £2.50

There are two painted versions of Puffin; on one the surface on which the bird stands is painted green to represent grass, and on the other it is yellow to represent sand.

DOE AND FAWN
Code: MC18
Issued: 1987
Retired: 1991
Issue Price: £2.50

TORTOISE

Code: MC25
Issued: 1987
Retired: 1989
Issue Price: £2.50

KOALA
(No picture available.)

Code: MC26
Issued: 1987
Retired: 1989
Issue Price: £2.50

BORDER COLLIE

Code: MC27
Issued: 1987
Retired: 1991
Issue Price: £2.50

BRACE OF PHEASANTS

Code: MC28
Issued: 1987
Retired: 1989
Issue Price: £2.50

LEAPING SALMON

Code: MC30
Issued: 1987
Retired: 1989
Issue Price: £2.50

GOLDEN EAGLE

Code: MC29
Issued: 1987
Retired: 1989
Issue Price: £2.50

FIELDVOLE AND WREN

Code: MC31
Issued: 1989
Retired: 1992
Issue Price: £3

RABBIT FAMILY

Code: MC32
Issued: 1989
Retired: 1990
Issue Price: £2.99

ROBIN

Code: MC33
Issued: 1989
Retired: 1991
Issue Price: £3

BARN OWL

Code: MC34
Issued: 1989
Retired: 1991
Issue Price: £3

CAT AND KITTENS

Code: MC35
Issued: 1989
Retired: 1991
Issue Price: £3

COCK AND HEN

Code: MC36
Issued: 1989
Retired: 1990
Issue Price: £3

Miniature Collection

69

Miniature Collection

RED SQUIRREL
Code: MC37
Issued: 1989
Retired: 1992
Issue Price: £3

PINE MARTENS
Code: MC38
Issued: 1989
Retired: 1992
Issue Price: £3

FOX AND CUBS
Code: MC39
Issued: 1989
Retired: 1992
Issue Price: £3

HIGHLAND COW AND CALF
Code: MC40
Issued: 1989
Retired: 1992
Issue Price: £3

STOAT
Code: MC41
Issued: 1989
Retired: 1991
Issue Price: £3

HARE
Code: MC42
Issued: 1989
Retired: 1992
Issue Price: £3

BADGER AND CUBS
Code: MC43
Issued: 1989
Retired: 1992
Issue Price: £3

BLUE TITS
Code: MC44
Issued: 1989
Retired: 1992
Issue Price: £3

KANGAROO
Code: MC45
Issued: 1989
Retired: 1992
Issue Price: £3

KINGFISHER
Code: MC46
Issued: 1989
Retired: 1992
Issue Price: £3

DORMOUSE
Code: MC47
Issued: 1989
Retired: 1992
Issue Price: £3

OTTER
Code: MC48
Issued: 1989
Retired: 1992
Issue Price: £3

This piece replaced the first Otter (MC8) which retired in 1989, and is smaller than the original. On some pieces, the otter is painted red, on others brown and green.

SEAL

Code: MC49
Issued: 1989
Retired: 1992
Issue Price: £3

SOAY RAM

Code: MC50
Issued: 1989
Retired: 1992
Issue Price: £3

WILD CAT

Code: MC51
Issued: 1989
Retired: 1992
Issue Price: £3

HARVEST MOUSE

Code: MC52
Issued: 1990
Retired: 1992
Issue Price: £4

EUROPEAN OWL

Code: MC53
Issued: 1990
Retired: 1992
Issue Price: £4

Code: MC54
Issued: 1990
Retired: 1992
Issue Price: £4

BULLFINCH

Code: MC55
Issued: 1990
Retired: 1992
Issue Price: £4

WOODPECKER

GREY SQUIRREL

Code: MC56
Issued: 1990
Retired: 1992
Issue Price: £4

Code: MC57
Issued: 1990
Retired: 1992
Issue Price: £4

GINGER KITTENS

GUN DOG

Code: MC58
Issued: 1990
Retired: 1992
Issue Price: £4

RETRIEVER AND PUPS

Code: MC59
Issued: 1990
Retired: 1992
Issue Price: £4

Miniature Collection

71

Hopscotch Minis

The Hopscotch Minis collection (sometimes referred to as just 'Hopscotch') have remained popular with collectors since their appearance in 1983 at the inception of Colour Box. As well as individual pieces, Hopscotch characters also frequently find their way onto Home Sweet Home sculptures, as ardent collectors will know! On occasions Hopscotch code numbers have been duplicated over the years (H7 = Goldfish, Monkey; H20 = Mouse, Seal; H22 = Brown Cow, Dormouse; H32 = Ladybird, Bumble Bee), and in one instance three pieces share the same number: H16 = Snake, Lion, Mouse. Although some pieces share the same name they may be an entirely different sculpture; for example, Badger H33 and H55 are quite different.

A complete set of the Hopscotch Collection, including two gilded hallmarked-silver miniatures made specially for the auction, were sold at Christie's in 1993 for £110.

STRIPED CAT (Ginger or Grey)

Code: H1
Issued: 1983
Issue Price: £1

Originally available only in ginger: alternative grey colouring was introduced in 1988.

PLAIN CAT

Code: H2
Issued: 1983
Retired: Spring 1995
Issue Price: £1

FROG

Code: H3
Issued: 1983
Issue Price: £1

ELEPHANT

Code: H4
Issued: 1983
Issue Price: £1

Originally available only in grey: alternative pink colouring was introduced in 1988.

DOG

Code: H5
Issued: 1983
Retired: 1989
Issue Price: £1

White with brown markings.

RABBIT

Code: H6
Issued: 1983
Issue Price: £1

GOLDFISH

Code: H7
Issued: 1983
Retired: 1985
Issue Price: £1

Goldfish is a very rare piece indeed — highly collectable.

MONKEY
(No picture available.)

Code: H7
Issued: 1985
Retired: 1987
Issue Price: £1

PIG

Code: H8
Issued: 1983
Issue Price: £1

DOG

Code: H9
Issued: 1983
Retired: 1989
Issue Price: £1

White with black markings.

BLACK CAT

Code: H10
Issued: 1983
Issue Price: £1

SHEEP

Code: H11
Issued: 1983
Retired: 1989
Issue Price: £1

DUCK

Code: H12
Issued: 1983
Issue Price: £1

Originally painted beige with a green head, but later changed to dark green/blue.

CAT ON BACK

Code: H13
Issued: 1983
Retired: 1989
Issue Price: £1

Originally painted ginger, but changed to grey in 1988.

CAMEL

Code: H14
Issued: 1983
Retired: 1987
Issue Price: £1

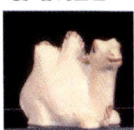

FAWN

Code: H14
Issued: 1987
Retired: 1989
Issue Price: £1

GREY RABBIT

Code: H15
Issued: 1983
Issue Price: £1

Now known as White Rabbit. The colour change was made in 1989.

Hopscotch Minis

73

Hopscotch Minis

SNAKE
Code: H16
Issued: 1983
Retired: 1985
Issue Price: £1

MOUSE
Code: H16
Issued: Mar 1987
Issue Price: £1

DOG (ON BACK)

Originally painted white with brown markings; later changed to mustard with white markings.

Code: H17
Issued: 1983
Retired: 1991
Issue Price: £1

LION

A very rare piece.

Code: H16
Issued: 1985
Retired: 1987
Issue Price: £1

HEDGEHOG
Code: H18
Issued: 1983
Issue Price: £1

SQUIRREL
Code: H19
Issued: 1983
Retired: 1989
Issue Price: £1

MOUSE
Code: H20
Issued: 1983
Retired: 1987
Issue Price: £1

SEAL
Code: H20
Issued: Mar 1987
Retired: 1989
Issue Price: £1

OWL
Code: H21
Issued: 1983
Issue Price: £1

BROWN COW
Code: H22 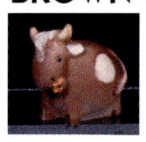
Issued: 1983
Retired: 1987
Issue Price: £1

DORMOUSE
Code: H22
Issued: Mar 1987
Retired: 1989
Issue Price: £1

HIPPO
Code: H23
Issued: 1983
Issue Price: £1

RABBIT ON BACK

Code: H24
Issued: 1983
Issue Price: £1

CAT

Code: H25
Issued: 1983
Retired: 1992
Issue Price: £1

Not to be confused with Cat (MC2) in the Miniature Collection: the pose of the cat is similar on both, but MC2 is peering at a mouse and is set on a circular base.

Code: H26
Issued: 1983
Retired: 1987
Issue Price: £1

DOVE

A very rare piece.

Code: H26
Issued: Mar 1987
Retired: 1989
Issue Price: £1

ROBIN

Very rare.

Code: H27
Issued: 1983
Retired: 1989
Issue Price: £1

DOG

Originally painted pinky beige with brown markings; later changed to white with brown markings.

Code: H28
Issued: 1983
Issue Price: £1

SLEEPING CAT

Code: H29
Issued: 1983
Retired: 1989
Issue Price: £1

KOALA

Very rare and much sought after by collectors.

Code: H30
Issued: 1983
Retired: 1989
Issue Price: £1

DOG

Originally painted brown: changed to black in 1987.

GREY CAT

Code: H31
Issued: 1986
Retired: Spring 1995
Issue Price: £1

A repainted version of Grey Cat was made in 1993 for the Bookmark — a gift to Collectors Club members who enrol a friend or relative. (The piece is attached to the bottom of the bookmark.)

LADYBIRD

Both H32 pieces (Ladybird and Bumble Bee) are very rare.

Code: H32
Issued: 1986
Retired: 1987
Issue Price: £1

Hopscatch Minis

Hopscotch Minis

BUMBLE BEE
Code: H32
Issued: Mar 1987
Retired: 1989
Issue Price: £1

BADGER
Code: H33 
Issued: 1986
Retired: 1989
Issue Price: £1

PIG ON BACK
Code: H34
Issued: 1986
Retired: 1992
Issue Price: £1

RECLINING PIG
Code: H35 
Issued: 1986
Retired: 1992
Issue Price: £1

RECLINING CAT
Code: H36
Issued: 1987
Retired: 1991
Issue Price: £1

FRIGHTENED CAT
Code: H37 
Issued: 1987
Retired: 1992
Issue Price: £1

BEGGING CAT
Code: H38
Issued: 1987
Retired: 1992
Issue Price: £1

WASHING CAT
Code: H39
Issued: 1987
Retired: 1992
Issue Price: £1

TEDDY BEAR (Pink or Blue Scarf)
Repainted version released in 1993.

Code: H40
Issued: 1987
Issue Price: £1

GUINEA PIG
Very rare and much sought after.

Code: H41
Issued: 1987
Retired: 1988
Issue Price: £1

HAMSTER
Hamster and Guinea Pig share the same code number, which is reasonable as they are the same piece painted differently!

Code: H41
Issued: 1988
Retired: 1989
Issue Price: £1

WHITE CAT
Repainted in 1988 to become Big Black Cat (also H42).

Code: H42
Issued: late 1987
Retired: 1988
Issue Price: £1

BIG BLACK CAT

Code: H42
Issued: 1988
Retired: 1992
Issue Price: £1

A repainted version of White Cat.

SHAGGY DOG

Code: H43
Issued: late 1987
Issue Price: £1

Repainted version released in 1993.

PENGUIN

Code: H44
Issued: 1989
Retired: 1991
Issue Price: £1.15

COCKEREL

Code: H45
Issued: 1989
Retired: 1991
Issue Price: £1.15

HEN

Code: H46
Issued: 1989
Retired: 1992
Issue Price: £1.15

BLUE TIT

Code: H47
Issued: 1989
Retired: 1992
Issue Price: £1.15

HEDGEHOG BEGGING

Code: H48
Issued: 1989
Retired: 1994
Issue Price: £1.15

SQUIRREL

Code: H49
Issued: 1989
Retired: 1991
Issue Price: £1.15

HARE

Code: H50
Issued: 1989
Retired: 1994
Issue Price: £1.15

DOLPHIN

Code: H51
Issued: 1989
Issue Price: £1.15

DUCKLING

Code: H52
Issued: 1989
Retired: Spring 1995
Issue Price: £1.15

FOX CUB

Code: H53
Issued: 1989
Issue Price: £1.15

Hopscotch Minis

BROWN BEAR

Code: H54
Issued: 1989
Retired: 1991
Issue Price: £1.15

BADGER

Code: H55
Issued: 1989
Retired: 1991
Issue Price: £1.15

SCOTTIE (White or Black)

Code: H57
Issued: 1989
Retired: 1991
Issue Price: £1.15

CAT AND BALL ▶

Code: H56
Issued: 1989
Retired: 1992
Issue Price: £1.15

Transferred in 1992 to Home Sweet Home as HS706. A version in solid sterling silver was also produced in 1989 for direct sale to Collectors Club members.

SHEEPDOG

Code: H58
Issued: 1989
Retired: 1994
Issue Price: £1.15

SHETLAND PONY

Code: H59
Issued: 1989
Retired: Spring 1995
Issue Price: £1.15

LAMB

Code: H60
Issued: 1989
Retired: Spring 1995
Issue Price: £1.15

SINGING CAT ▶

Code: H61
Issued: 1991
Retired: 1992
Issue Price: £1.15

Transferred in 1992 to Home Sweet Home collection as HS706.

CAT AND WOOL ▶

Code: H62
Issued: 1991
Retired: 1992
Issue Price: £1.15

Transferred to Home Sweet Home as HS702.

CAT AND FISHBONE

Code: H63
Issued: 1991
Retired: 1992
Issue Price: £1.15

Transferred to Home Sweet Home as HS703

CAT AND TOY MOUSE

Code: H64
Issued: 1991
Retired: 1992
Issue Price: £1.15

Transferred to Home Sweet Home as HS704

Hopscotch minis

CAT AND BOW

Code: H65
Issued: 1991
Retired: 1992
Issue Price: £1.15

Transferred to Home Sweet Home as HS705

DOG AND BONE

Code: H66
Issued: 1991
Retired: 1992
Issue Price: £1.15

GORILLA

Code: H67
Issued: Mar 1992
Retired: 1994
Issue Price: £1.15

DONKEY

Code: H68
Issued: Mar 1992
Issue Price: £1.15

SNAKES ALIVE

Code: H69
Issued: Mar 1992
Retired: Spring 1995
Issue Price: £1.15

POLAR BEAR

Code: H70
Issued: Mar 1992
Issue Price: £1.15

SEAL

Code: H71
Issued: Mar 1992
Issue Price: £1.15

PANDA SITTING

Code: H72
Issued: Jun 1992
Issue Price: £1.15

LION

Code: H73
Issued: Jun 1992
Issue Price: £1.15

PANDA RECLINING

Code: H74
Issued: Jun 1992
Retired: Spring 1995
Issue Price: £1.15

ALLIGATOR

Code: H75
Issued: Jun 1992
Retired: 1994
Issue Price: £1.15

MONKEY

Code: H76
Issued: Jun 1992
Retired: Spring 1995
Issue Price: £1.15

Hopscotch Minis

Hopscotch Minis

PARROT
Code: H77
Issued: Jun 1992
Issue Price: £1.15

LEOPARD
Code: H78
Issued: Jun 1992
Retired: Spring 1995
Issue Price: £1.15

PATTY
Code: H79
Issued: Sept 1993
Retired: Spring 1995
Issue Price: £1.15

The first of a collection of six dinosaurs (H79-84), released in response to the dinosaur mania created by Steven Spielberg's film 'Jurassic Park'. The names are abbreviations of the real dinosaur names they represent (e.g. Tricey = Triceratops).

DIMEY
Code: H80 
Issued: Sept 1993
Retired: Spring 1995
Issue Price: £1.15

TYRO
Code: H81
Issued: Sept 1993
Retired: Spring 1995
Issue Price: £1.15

PARRY
Code: H82
Issued: Sept 1993
Retired: Spring 1995
Issue Price: £1.15

TRICEY
Code: H83 
Issued: Sept 1993
Retired: Spring 1995
Issue Price: £1.15

STEGGY
Code: H84
Issued: Sept 1993
Retired: Spring 1995
Issue Price: £1.15

MR NOAH
Code: H85
Issued: Sept 1993
Retired: Spring 1995
Issue Price: £1.15

MRS NOAH
Code: H86
Issued: Sept 1993
Retired: Spring 1995
Issue Price: £1.15

CARDY
Code: H87
Issued: Mar 1994
Issue Price: £1.15

MACAWLEY

Code: H88
Issued: Mar 1994
Issue Price: £1.15

EAGERLY

Code: H89
Issued: Mar 1994
Issue Price: £1.15

LOONEY TOUCAN

Code: H90
Issued: Mar 1994
Issue Price: £1.15

COCKATOONEY

Code: H91
Issued: Mar 1994
Issue Price: £1.15

DO-DO

Code: H92
Issued: Mar 1994
Issue Price: £1.15

TINY TED (Pink)

Code: H94
Issued: Feb 1995
Issue Price: £1.15

TINY TED (Blue)

Code: H93
Issued: Feb 1995
Issue Price: £1.15

SNAIL

Code: H96
Issued: Feb 1995
Issue Price: £1.15

SLEEPING HEDGHOG

Code: H95
Issued: Feb 1995
Issue Price: £1.15

Hopscotch Minis

81

Pennywhistle Lane

An entirely new collection, Pennywhistle Lane was released in 1993, the tenth year of Colour Box. Like the Teddy Bears Collection, the central figurine characters are based on real toys owned by Peter Fagan. He has transported them into an imaginary setting based upon the notion of "what you might discover in the attic of an old, once deserted cottage" — dolls, teddies, toys and an assortment of fascinating bric-a-brac, not to mention a family of mice! The first piece in the collection, The Attic, is the home of all the characters, and is the first part of a model of the whole of Number One Pennywhistle Lane that Peter plans to sculpt room by room.

The mice who live in the attic are called the Whistlers and they, together with all the other characters, have stories to tell, courtesy of Frances Fagan.

THE ATTIC

The attic in question belongs to Number One Pennywhistle Lane and the roof on the piece is typical of those to be found on the south-east coast of Scotland and the very north-east coast of England (where Peter now lives). A special commemorative coin, struck by the Royal Mint, was given away with the first 500 pieces to be sold. The coins are close in size, weight, design and metal to the predecimal one penny piece and were presented in a box bearing the Royal Crest.

Code: PL001
Issued: Sept 1993
Issue Price: £249.50

Code: PL002
Issued: Feb 1995
Issue Price: £175

THE BEDROOM

Code: PL099
Issued: Mar 1994
Issue Price: £10.50

PENNYWHISTLE LANE WALL

The local council usually have the responsibility to paint the Pennywhistle Lane Roadsign. Every year men in white overalls come with paint pots and do the job very well. But this year was an exception. The Whistlers had been waiting for several months for the van to come and for the sign to receive its usual freshen-up, but no luck! So the Whistlers took it upon themselves to put matters right and late one evening, they ventured out to engineer the job for themselves!

Code: PL102
Issued: Sept 1993
Issue Price: £21.95

PIANO RAG

*I*t takes a lot of energy for a Pennywhistle mouse to play a tune on the old attic piano. After all, he has to jump about to achieve true harmony and even then it's easy to step on a wrong note!

ROUND THE TREE

Code: PL103
Issued: Jul 1994
Issue Price: £65.50

*A*t the centre of all Christmas celebrations is the tree. It is dressed in every treasure that the Whistler mice can find. They search high and low throughout the year and often venture out of the Pennywhistle attic to find extra gifts which are kept secret until the night before Christmas. On this special day they are the busiest of all, hurrying to decorate the tree and every year they try to make it better than the year before.
This piece had the working title Christmas Melody.

THE WHISTLERS' NATIVITY

*I*n the quiet of Christmas Eve, the mice are preparing their Nativity play. The Whistlers all gather together and choose their parts. Each year Angelina and Gloria Whistler volunteer to play the angels. The part of Mary and Joseph change each year and the baby must always be the smallest Whistler who can manage to fit into the crib.
This piece had the working title Nativity Scene.

Code: PL104
Issued: Jul 1994
Issue Price: £21.50

Pennywhistle Lane

83

PASSING TIME

Code: PL201
Issued: Sept 1993
Issue Price: £13.95

Mice are forever running up clocks if we are all to believe in the nursery rhymes. What is seldom recorded is the fact that if small fat mice run up clocks, they are just as likely to fall down again and land at the bottom with a bump. It's the pendulum that the mice like best and when the clock starts ticking the pendulum makes a perfect swing. Sometimes the baby mice are hung on the pendulum in their cradles when they won't go to sleep!

INDOOR GARDEN

Code: PL202
Issued: Sept 1993
Retired: Spring 1995
Issue Price: £11.95

An old plant pot holder that used to house a small fern was tumbled up into the attic after it got cracked and started to leak. Pennywhistle mice have a talent for turning the most useless junk into handy hidey-holes or usable tools and here they are busy sorting out the bits and pieces to put in the pot in case they come in useful.

OLD SEA SALT

Code: PL203
Issued: March 1994
Issue Price: £13.95

Though his days of salty travels are over, Sam the Monkey could never be parted from his seafarer's trunk full of past treasures which now stay with him on his canal trips in the Netherlands.

NIGHT NURSE

If you're feeling poorly and a little bit feverish, you'll need a night nurse to help you get better. Of course the baby mice do catch cold easily being so small but there's always a soothing paw for comfort and some strong herbal tea being brewed.

Code: PL301
Issued: Sept 1993
Retired: Spring 1995
Issue Price: £8.95

SEE-SAW

Code: PL302
Issued: Sept 1993
Issue Price: £7.95

The baby mice in Pennywhistle Lane are never still for more than a minute. They turn any kind of leftover treasures into games and this time it took three mice to even lift the old ruler onto the jar to make the see-saw. They manage very well despite weighing so little themselves and a big push is all it takes to set the see-saw moving.

SHOE HOUSE

Code: PL303
Issued: Sept 1993
Retired: Spring 1995
Issue Price: £7.95

One of the best hiding places in the attic for the Pennywhistle Lane mice is grandad's old garden shoe. For years and years he refused to throw them both away although they were well worn out. Even though he doesn't know, grandad would be pleased that his old shoe has come in useful after all. A colourway of Shoe House, adapted as a hanging ornament and renamed Santa's Boot, is available in the USA. The USA version also has a different storyline: *The Whistler mice in Peter Fagan's attic found this old boot one year soon after Christmas. It was such a wonderful colour that they believed it must have been Santa Claus' own boot that fell off when he was coming down the chimney! The attic toys knew that Santa would never have left his boot behind, but the mice seemed so pleased with their new treasure that they didn't want to spoil their story.*

PENNYWHISTLE EXPRESS

Code: PL304
Issued: Sept 1993
Retired: Spring 1995
Issue Price: £7.95

There is only one place in the Universe where train timetables don't matter and that is the magical world of Pennywhistle Lane. Of course, any train driven by a Pennywhistle mouse has got to be considering magic and, therefore, a timetable probably isn't the most important consideration. However, the driver has to be aware of his responsibilities and the Pennywhistle Express needs to leave on time.

COTTAGE CHEESE

Code: PL305
Issued: Sept 1993
Retired: Spring 1995
Issue Price: £7.95

Everybody knows mice love cheese but only the Pennywhistle mice insist on having it from the old cheese dish. Nobody really knows how the cheese dish got broken but once the corner had been knocked off it made an ideal hiding place for small mice with a passion for hide and seek.

TUCKED UP TIGHT

Code: PL306
Issued: Mar 1994
Issue Price: £7.95

In the Pennywhistle Attic the mice find very unusual places to spend the night. This baby Whistler mouse is fast asleep in an old drawer from a doll's cabinet. It's just the right size for a comfy, cosy bed.

OLD TIME MUSIC

Some of the Whistlers have special musical skills. Others appreciate a good tune or sing along with the old time music that they play on the tiny doll's gramophone which they found in the toy box. The mice like the dance tunes best when everyone gets the chance to join in and let their hair down, especially if there is a birthday to celebrate or just any excuse to have a party!

Code: PL307
Issued: Mar 1994
Issue Price: £7.95

BEDTIME TALES

Just before all the toys in the attic go to sleep on Christmas Eve, when the clock strikes seven, the Whistler mice get ready. They bring down their special story book from the top shelf and open it at their favourite story, the story of Christmas. As they open the pages and begin the well-known tale, the other mice enact the pageant in preparation for the special night that is to follow.

Code: PL308
Issued: Jul 1994
Issue Price: £7.95

WICKER WORK

It's always a last minute rush for the Whistler mice in Peter Fagan's attic as they prepare their gifts for all their friends. It takes a long time for such tiny mice to wrap all their shopping and they always make use of last year's paper which they use again as Whistler mice never waste anything that might come in useful. They are, therefore, always careful when they open their presents so they don't tear the paper.

Code: PL309
Issued: Jul 1994
Issue Price: £7.95

TOBY

Bounding with energy and falling over himself with the desire to join in, Toby the wire-haired terrier dog simply cannot be left out of any games. There were times when he had been mislaid amongst the other toys in the trunk where he lived but his uncanny knack of squeezing his way out of any corner always found him on top and simply desperate to be included.

Code: PL401
Issued: Sept 1993
Retired: Spring 1995
Issue Price: £13.95

BILLY

Code: PL402
Issued: Sept 1993
Issue Price: £11.95

Billy used to have a real Nanny. She always knew best and Billy did everything she said. He lived in the nursery with lots of other toys and was what Nanny called a "Sunday Doll". That meant he was only played with on Sundays and special times like Birthdays and Christmas.

JANGLES THE JESTER

A scatter of magic dust was all that it took to make Jangles burst into life. His history was anybody's guess. He liked to tell stories about he Court of King Arthur. He recalled days in an acrobatic troupe who toured around the provinces in distant lands, but mostly he told of the fairground and the magic sounds of the music machine called The Polyphon.

Code: PL403
Issued: Sept 1993
Issue Price: £11.95

JANGLES JUGGLING

Code: PL404
Issued: Jul 1994
Issue Price: £11.95

Jangles the Jester is famous for his story-telling. He has a long history of exciting adventures and takes every opportunity to recount the magical happenings from his past lives. On his travels he had learned how to juggle the magical spangled clubs and balls and often performed his tricks to royal households. On one notable occasion he had even juggled for the King of Siam who claimed he was the best of all the performing troubadours.

TRINKET'S DRUM

Trinket the Bear was never very sure of himself. He found he got in a muddle too easily and often needed a helping hand. Before Trinket came to live in Peter Fagan's Pennywhistle Lane attic he spent most of his time in a toy box in a cupboard, where he was put away until the school holidays. The children who used to live in his house went to boarding school and weren't there every day to play with the toys. Trinket used to sit with the other toys desperate for time to pass quickly so he would be brought out for new adventures . . .

Code: PL405
Issued: Jul 1994
Issue Price: £11.95

MOUSE HOUSE

Code: PL406
Issued: Feb 1995
Issue Price: £11.95

Pennywhistle Lane

87

Pennywhistle Lane

BECCY

Code: PL501
Issued: Sept 1993
Issue Price: £11.95

There is a dream in every little girl's heart that one day she will be a famous dancer. Beccy knew that because she was only a china doll she could never be a real dancer but she dreamed about it nonetheless. She didn't want to be a ballerina; she wanted to be one of those bright music hall girls in a frilly petticoat and garter. She dreamed of shining lights and loud music and solo singers who performed nightly at the theatre.

GOLLY & TRINKET

Code: PL502
Issued: Sept 1993
Issue Price: £8.95

Dependable and friendly, Golly loves to have plenty to do and surrounds himself with activity! He helps Trinket the bear to sort out his muddles in the toy box and is best solving puzzles and lifting the worries of the other Pennywhistle toys in Peter Fagan's attic. Golly loves entertaining the toys with stories and acrobatics and everyone wants him to join them in their games.

SAM

Code: PL503
Issued: Sept 1993
Issue Price: £8.95

Sam has seen it all in his time, which makes him an ideal character to advise the other attic toys. He lived for years on an old Dutch barge and spent most of his life in transit. He hasn't seen all the world but he has read so many books that his knowledge and experience provide comfort and advice to anyone who needs his help.

SOCKY & TITCH

Code: PL504
Issued: March 1994
Issue Price: £8.95

Socky, the elephant, is so called because he was once a pair of grey school socks and hails from the days when toys were scarce and money for toys even more scarce. When an old pair of hand-knitted socks got beyond repair they were painstakingly unpicked, the wool was washed and skeined and nimble fingers got to work to create something new. Socky is rather shy about his size, but he has found a golly to be his friend.

GOLLY SITTING

Code: PL505
Issued: Mar 1994
Issue Price: £8.95

Dependable and friendly, Golly loves to have plenty to do and surrounds himself with activity! He helps Trinket the bear to sort out his muddles in the toy box and is best at solving puzzles and lifting the worries of the other Pennywhistle toys in Peter Fagan's attic. Golly loves entertaining the toys with stories and acrobatics and everyone wants him to join in their games.

SECRET PRESENTS

Code: PL506
Issued: Jul 1994
Issue Price: £8.95

Christmas is always a time for secrets and whether it's wrapping or unwrapping the festive packages, the attic mice always enjoy themselves. The best part of the surprise is to watch the faces of the baby mice when they open the boxes and see what Santa has brought. It isn't easy for the mice to go shopping, so they spend the whole year saving special found gifts and hiding them away until Christmas Eve. Then the paper and string come out and the fun begins.
This piece had the working title Surprise Parcel

THREE WISE MICE

Code: PL507
Issued: Jul 1994
Issue Price: £8.95

No Nativity would be complete without the arrival of the Three Kings. and Christmas celebrations in the attic reach their height when the mice perform the Nativity play for the other toys. The tallest and most regal of the mice play the part of the Three Wise Men and they bring gifts th the sleeping baby in the manger. Found gifts are always better than expensive offerings and the mice pay homage with their tiny attic treasures.

WINSTON PODMORE

Code: PL508
Issued: Jul 1994
Issue Price: £8.95

Winston Podmore arrived in the attic at Pennywhistle Lane more by luck than by judgement when his hot air balloon made a surprise crash landing on the roof! He has dreamt of being an aviator ever since he was a piglet but he was always told that pigs can't fly. Being VERY determined, he decided that the place he was most at home was in the air and he didn't really mind just how he got there. Winston has tried most methods of becoming airborne, from ballooning to flying machines. It's lucky that he likes parachuting too as coming down is sometimes easier than going up!

ROCK A BYE

Code: PL509
Issued: Feb 1995
Issue Price: £8.95

Pennywhistle Lane

89

MUMMY & WEENY WHISTLER

Hush! In the darkness of the Attic, there's a squeak and a patter. Could it be the tiny feet have shoes on? Surely not! Listen again and close your eyes tight and if you wish hard enough you'll see them running in the shadows. The glimmer of a tiny top hat, the flicker of a red ribbon, only the very gifted can see the mice in the Pennywhistle Attic are dressed and ready for an outing. But how do mice dress? Smartly, of course, and in perfect miniature — such tiny buttons and gloves! The Whistlers live in Pennywhistle Lane. They are the mice who have always been there. They live amongst the attic junk and make their homes in other people's bric-a-brac. Meet all the Whistler family of mice. Close your eyes tightly, wish a little harder and you'll see them too! (This generic introduction also accompanies all Pennywhistle Lane figurines in the Whistler family — PL602, PL603, PL604, PL605, PL606, PL607, PL608.)

Code: PL601
Issued: Sept 1993
Retired: Spring 1995
Issue Price: £3.95

NANNY & WINKIE WHISTLER

Code: PL602
Issued: Sept 1993
Retired: Spring 1995
Issue Price: £3.95

Code: PL603
Issued: Sept 1993
Issue Price: £2.99

JUNIOR WHISTLER

GREAT UNCLE WHISTLER

Code: PL604
Issued: Sept 1993
Issue Price: £2.99

MISSY WHISTLER

Code: PL605
Issued: Sept 1993
Issue Price: £3.95

UNCLE WILLIAM'S VISIT

Code: PL606
Issued: Mar 1994
Issue Price: £3.95

AUNTY & WENDY WHISTLER

Code: PL607
Issued: Mar 1994
Issue Price: £2.95

Code: PL609
Issued: Jul 1994
Issue Price: £3.95

SISSY WHISTLER

Code: PL608
Issued: Mar 1994
Issue Price: £2.95

THE CHOIR ▶

This piece had the working title Choir Boys.

Code: PL610
Issued: Jul 1994
Issue Price: £3.95

THE HEAVENLY HOST

In the quiet of Peter Fagan's Attic, just before the Whistler mice enact the Christmas pageant for the toys, there is a moment of quiet for the tiniest celebration of Christmas. Two baby Whistlers dress as angels and sing the first verse of that favourite carol, 'Silent Night'. Their voices are so quiet and true that all the toys are, for a moment, quite still. Nothing or no-one so small could send quite such an important message of peace on this special might.
This piece had the working title Angel Chorus.

Code: PL700
Issued: Feb 1995
Issue Price: £17.95

PERSONAL VALET

DRESSING TABLE

Code: PL701
Issued: Feb 1995
Issue Price: £17.95

BEDTIME

Code: PL800
Issued: Feb 1995
Issue Price: £16.75

CHAISE LONGUE

Code: PL802
Issued: Feb 1995
Issue Price: £16.75

Pennywhistle Lane

91

Colour Box in the USA

Since 1994 Peter Fagan's sculptures have been marketed in the USA by the Enesco Corporation under the name Pennywhistle Lane, which replaced the previous name used prior till then — 'Adorables'. The collection consists mainly of the UK Pennywhistle Lane collection but includes a) selected pieces from other collections, some in colourway versions and some adapted from the originals; b) a few specially created items not currently available in the UK. Known details of US colourways are given here. Some Teddies are also available as a separate collection under the name 'Centimental Bears'. Home Sweet Home cats are due to be launched under their own range name in 1996. Unless stated otherwise, all the pieces listed here are also available in other countries worldwide.

1994 RELEASES

Gustav and Christopher
Both bears hold a cushion-shaped heart inscribed with the words 'BEARS MEAN LOVE'. Available only in the USA.

Night Nurse
Code: 128635

Socky and Titch
Code: 128651

The Whistlers' Nativity
Code: 654973
Issue Price: $40.00

The Choir Boys
Code: 654981
Issue Price: $5.00

The Three Wise Mice
Code: 655007
Issue Price: $10.00

Round The Tree
Code: 655015
Issue Price: $65.00

Santa Paws
Code: 655023
Issue Price: $10.00
Different coloured presents in sack (UK version retired in 1993).

The Heavenly Host
Code: 655031
Issue Price: $.00

Christmas Correspondent
Code: 655325
Issue Price: $10.00
A modified and renamed version of The Correspondent, with Christmas Cards in the letter rack and a pink envelope in the cat's mouth.

Pennywhistle Express
Code: 655333
Issue Price: $10.00

Christmas Carol
Code: 655341
Issue Price: $10.00
Retired in the UK in 1993.

Quiet Moments
Code: 655368
Issue Price: $30.00
A doll sitting in a chair. This piece is not currently (1995) available in the UK.

Popsey
Code: 655376
Issue Price: $10.00
Not the same as the UK piece called Popsey (retired in 1994) but a renamed, unchanged version of Party Bear (retired in the UK in 1993).

Trinkets Drum
Code: 655384
Issue Price: $15.00

James
Code: 655392
Issue Price: $10.00
Not the same piece as the UK piece with the same name (which retired in 1994) but a renamed, unchanged version of Present Time (retired in the UK in 1993).

Juggling Jangles
Code: 655406
Issue Price: $15.00

Passing Time
Code: 655414
Issue Price: $17.50

Hanging Ornaments
Code: 655422
Issue Price: $12.50 each
Three of the four ornaments are adaptions of UK pieces — Shoe House, Wicker Work and Bedtime Tales. The fourth, a gold spinning top with mice on, has no UK equivalent.

Secret Presents
Code: 655430
Issue Price: $12.50

Jack-In-The-Box
Code: 655499
Issue Price: $12.50
Dickie Bear replaced by a mouse (UK version retired in 1993).

The Attic
Code: 657808
Issue Price: $300.00

Great Uncle Whistler
Code: 657816
Issue Price: $5.00

Afternoon Stroll
Code: 657824
Issue Price: $17.50

Toby
Code: 657832
Issue Price: $17.50

Piano Rag
Code: 657859
Issue Price: $50.00
The US version is a modification of the UK piece and is a 'barrel piano' (or player piano or pianola, with the addition of a piano roll instead of a music desk.

Billy
Code: 657883
Issue Price: $15.00

See-Saw
Code: 657891
Issue Price: $10.00

Bookworm
Code: 657905
Issue Price: $10.00
Books painted red and blue.

Ben
Code: 657948
Issue Price: $5.00
Red ribbon round medal.

Davey
Code: 657956
Issue Price: $5.00
Red, yellow & blue striped waistcoat.

Sam
Code: 658006
Issue Price: $10.00

Beccy
Code: 658014
Issue Price: $10.00

Mummy's Girl
Code: 657840
Issue Price: $5.00

Mummy & Weeny Whistler
Code: 657875
Issue Price: $5.00

Lots of Luck
Code: 657913
Issue Price: $5.00

Binky
Code: 657921
Issue Price: $5.00
Green/white striped jumper with red buttons: also spelling variation (in error) — in the UK he's Binkie.

Prudence
Code: 657964
Issue Price: $10.00
Mid-blue ribbons on dress and black ribbon round hat.

Stanley
Code: 657972
Issue Price: $10.00

George
Code: 657980
Issue Price: $10.00
Red waistcoat with blue/green embroidery and yellow buttons.

Jangles The Jester
Code: 657999
Issue Price: $10.00

Pennywhistle Lane Roadsign
Code: 657867
Issue Price: $25.00
An adapted version of the UK version (Pennywhistle Wall) with a second plaque which reads 'FROM ENESCO'.

1995 RELEASES

Priscilla
Code: 114367

Jingles Better
Code: 127892

Prima Ballerina
Code: 128643

Christmas Cat
Code: 145106
Hanging ornament.

Letter to Santa
Code: 145114
Retired in the UK 1991.

Personal Valet
Code: 145378

Bedtime
Code: 145386

Lighting Up Time
Code: 145408

Dressing Table
Code: 145424

Cat Basket
Code: 145394
Lilac pillow. (UK version with a blue pillow retired in 1992.)

Chaise Longue
Code: 145416

Rock-A-Bye
Code: 145432

Mouse House
Code: 145440

The Bedroom
Code: 145556

Bear Back Rider
Code: 151106

Trunk of Teddies
A limited edition of 1,000. (Release in the UK planned for 1996.)

Winter Sport

August String-Bear
(Retired in the UK in 1993.)

CENTIMENTAL BEARS

1994

Peter Bear
Code: 116289
Red scarf.

Arabella
Code: 116300

Timmy
Code: 116327

Regina
Code: 116343
Pink dress and boots.

Kenny
Code: 116351

Ian
Code: 116513
White bow with red spots.

Elly May
Code: 116521

Jilly
Code: 116548

Morris Minor
Code: 116785

Chocolate Chip
Code: 116807

Joseph
Code: 116823

Teddy Robinson
Code: 116831

Bernard
Code: 116947

Clarissa
Code: 117374

Burt
Code: 122378
Red shirt with Underground badge.

William
Code: 122386

The Happy Couple
Code: 122440

Miranda
Code: 122424

Jack
Code: 122416

Violet
Code: 125717

Adrian
Code: 125725

1995

Nym's Black Cat
Code: 145122

Binkie's Pumpkin
Code: 145130

Meekie's Lantern
Code: 145149

Spooky Ralph
Code: 145157

Sopwith Gets Ready
Code: 145165

Wizard Litmus
Code: 145173

Reggy The Halloween Bandit
Code: 145181

Irvine's Trick or Treat
Code: 145203

On The Ice
Code: 145238
Hanging ornament.

Just For You
Code: 145246
Hanging ornament.

Squidge
Code: 145254

Baron Von Berne
Code: 145262

Sullivan
Code: 145270

Ollie
Code: 145289

Mr Perkins
Code: 145297

Vernon
Code: 145300

Red Bear
Code: 145319

Emlyn
Code: 145327

Cousin Eccy
Code: 145335

Bruno
Code: 145343

The Collectors Club & Limited Editions

THE COLOUR BOX COLLECTORS CLUB

Launched in 1987, the Colour Box Collectors Club was initially administered by Jane and Dave Allan, friends of Peter Fagan's, who also ran a smallholding in the Borders. They produced a modest black & white newsletter called The Colour Box Collector, corresponded with collectors and organised the despatch of Club pieces and offers.

The Club was a success from the start. Member No.1, Mark Peck, was recruited in June 1987, and such was the speed at which membership increased that in early 1990 Susan Hargreaves became the 10,000th member. In early 1995 the total number of recruits was well on its way to 50,000.

The first colour newsletter appeared in summer 1989 and it was about this time that the Allans relinquished control of a Club which had become administratively very demanding. Peter Fagan's wife Frances had been helping with Club matters from the beginning, contributing articles for the newsletter and corresponding with collectors, and now she became editor of the newsletter and has also overseen the management of the Collectors Club ever since. Being so close to Peter there could be no better person to offer an insight into his work.

In 1991 the newsletter transformed into a magazine proper with 24 glossy pages of news, information and competitions for collectors. It also acquired a name — Collections and Reflections — chosen from collectors suggestions in a competition in the newsletter. For the first time the magazine was also made available to non-Club members with a cover price of £1.00. In March 1995 the magazine increased to 32 pages.

Probably the greatest attractions of Club membership are the complimentary gift piece and the opportunity to purchase pieces sculpted by Peter Fagan exclusively for Club members.

CLUB PIECES

Listed here are the pieces offered to Club members as a complimentary gift on either joining for the first time or renewing their membership. However, 1995/96 heralds a new idea which breaks with this established tradition — see Opening Night.

BLACKBOARD

Blackboard also exists as a shop point of sale (see section on Other Items) and features Hopscotch characters Plain Cat (H2) and Teddy Bear (H40).

Code: CC87
Issued: June 1987
Retired: May 1988

EASEL

Issued: June 1988
Retired: May 1989

95

ATTIC

Issued: June 1989
Retired: May 1990

The old picture frame is one Peter remembers used to be stored higgledepiggledy with other pieces of bric-a-brac in the family loft.

NOTICE BOARD

At the bottom of the lane where Peter lived as a boy was the old church, on the little village green. On the edge of the green stood the Parish Notice Board with news and happenings in the village pinned up for all to see. This is Peter's memory of the board, complete with his pet cat, a cheeky little bird and Johann bear.

WALL

Issued: June 1990
Retired: May 1991

The wall in question is the wall that surrounded the big house where one of Peter's boyhood friends, Morris, lived. Peter would visit Morris every weekend, and part of the four mile journey involved a short cut over 'the wall'. Note the broken bricks that made excellent footholds!

Issued: June 1991
Retired: May 1992

CHALKBOARD

This piece takes Peter back to his own primary school days in Essex. He was never very academic but in his first school report his headmistress said he was very good with plasticine and enjoyed modelling!

Issued: June 1992
Retired: May 1993

BILLBOARD

Peter used to do a paper round years ago, and every morning he would lean his bike on the old billboard outside the local paper shop. Although Peter's little dog wasn't quite the same breed as the puppy in this piece, he used to hide under the old billboard in just the same way. Also hiding under the billboard is Tinker Thomas.

Issued: June 1993
Retired: May 1994

OPENING NIGHT

Issued: June 1994
Retired: May 1996

There are two mould versions of this piece. In Mould 1 the diamonds on the curtains are painted on freehand, whereas in Mould 2 they are cut into the mould as a guide for homepainters. The first version is also more elaborately painted, with flowers on the stage, multicoloured letters in the word 'Collections' and patterns on either side of the words 'Peter Fagan'. These are all missing on the second version.

Opening Night is the complimentary piece for all Club members (new and renewing) between June 1994 and May 1995. It is also the complimentary piece for *new* members joining between June '95 and May '96. However, *renewing* members for the '95/'96 year have the choice of three pieces, one for each of the main collections of Teddy Bears, Home Sweet Home and Pennywhistle Lane. Collectors who would like to add more than one to their collection can purchase the other two at cost price.

FELINE FROLICS
Renewal item for Home Sweet Home collectors: June 1995 - May 1996

LEARNER DRIVER
Renewal item for Pennywhistle Lane collectors: June 1995 - May 1996

CLUB OFFERS

Club Offers are pieces offered for purchase exclusively by Collectors Club members. The first three items (two specially sculpted pieces, Decorative Cat and Theodore's Pastimes, and the Silver Miniatures) were made available directly from the Colour Box Club Office. Thereafter pieces have been ordered from retailers by presenting a Redemption Certificate supplied with the Club newsletter/magazine.

DECORATIVE CAT

Issued: Summer 1988
Issue Price: £12

The first special Club piece for Home Sweet Home collectors, featuring a cat having some fun with Christmas decorations, was presented on a wooden plinth.

SILVER MINIATURES

Two models from the Hopscotch Collection were produced in solid sterling silver — Mini Teddy and Cat & Ball (pictured here).

Issued: 1989
Issue Price: Cat & Ball £25; Mini Teddy £21.

MOTHER'S PRIDE

A 'mother' complete with litter of mischievous kittens. This was the first Collectors Club special piece to be available through stockists using the redemption certificate system. Decorative Cat, Theodore's Pastimes and the Silver Miniatures were all sold direct from the Club Office.

Issued: 1991
Retired: 1992
Issue Price: £12
Edition Size: 3,000

DRESSING TABLE

Featuring a very self-conscious puss admiring herself in the mirror! As 1992 was a leap year, the moulds for this piece were destroyed on 29th February.

Issued: 1991
Retired: 1992
Issue Price: £13

PICNIC PUSS

Two mischievous felines can be seen creating havoc with an al fresco lunch!

Issued: Apr 1992
Retired: Mar 1992
Issue Price: £20

DOLLS HOUSE

Code: CC930S
Issued: Apr 1993
Retired: Mar 1994
Issue Price: £24.99

LAUNDRY PUPS

Due to an "administrative error", Laundry Pups has the same code number as Sopwith's Solo Flight (the 93/94 Club piece for Teddy collectors).

Code: CC932S
Issued: Apr 1993
Retired: Mar 1994
Issue Price: £19.99

PRIVATE ENTRANCE

Code: CC933S
Issued: Apr 1994
Retired: Mar 1995
Issue Price: £50

The back door in Peter's boyhood home in Essex was the inspiration for this clever piece — note the cat halfway through the cat flap, body on one side, tail on the other! The back door of the same house appears in another piece — Doorstep Dilemma. Private Entrance is presented in a silk lined presentation box with a certificate of authenticity.

An entire collection of Collectors Club pieces available between 1987 and 1993, comprising seven annual Club joining pieces, two solid sterling silver miniature figurines and eleven Limited Edition pieces were sold as one lot at the 1993 Christie's auction for £220.

Code: CC935
Issued: April 1994-March 1996
Issue Price: £19.95

THE HEAD GARDENER ▶

THE TOY TRUNK

Code: CC936
Issued: April 1995-March 1996

A club offer for Pennywhistle Lane collectors.
(Picture not available prior to publication)

club and Limited Editions

ADDITIONAL ITEMS

BOOK MARKS
Issued: June 1992

A choice of six Colour Box book marks were introduced in 1992 as a free gift for Club members who enrol a friend. Each book mark features a tie on animal from the Hopscotch collection in a special colourway version. Between June and Christmas 1992 all book marks issued were signed by Peter Fagan.

LIMITED EDITIONS

The following pieces have been issued by Colour Box in pre-announced limited editions.

FESTIVE HOPSCOTCH PIECES

Issued: 1990
Edition Size: 750
Issue Price: £2 each or £18 per set.

Ten Hopscotch pieces painted in suitably festive colours and supplied with a mini gift bag and matching gift tag.

Polar Bear, Christmas Cat, Festive Cat and Ball, Festive Penguin, White Dog, Snowman, White Sleeping Cat, Arctic Hare, Arctic Fox, Snowy Ted.

A complete set of the Festive Hopscotch pieces was sold at the 1993 Christie's auction and fetched £352.

Code: HSL01
Issued: Sept 1993
Edition Size: 1,500
Issue Price: £100

MOONLIGHT SERENADE

Moonlight Serenade was sculpted to celebrate the tenth anniversary year of Colour Box and each piece is supplied with a numbered certificate. Technically the piece was difficult to produce and it was six months before it was able to go into production. The lampost was the problem; it eventually had to be cast in metal.

THE MUSIC OF THE POLYPHON

Code: PL101
Issued: Sept 1993
Edition Size: 1,500
Issue Price: £80

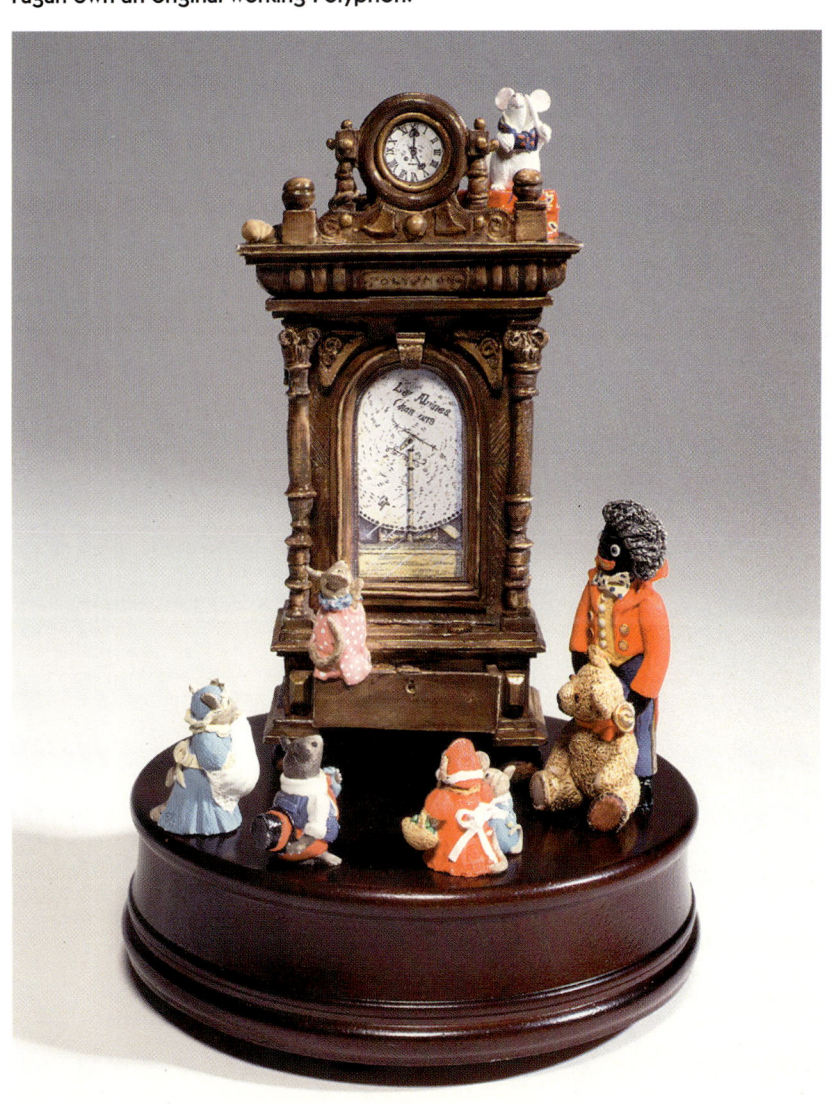

This is the first Colour Box musical piece; the wooden base contains a clockwork mechanism wound by a key. Each piece is presented in a silk-lined box with its own numbered certificate. A Polyphon is a Victorian music box operated by dropping a coin in a slot. As the music plays, a metal disc can be seen turning slowly through the glass front. Peter and Frances Fagan own an original working Polyphon.

Other Items

ARTHUR THE CAT COLLECTION

Arthur is of course the famous cat, star of TV, who had Arthur's the cat food renamed after him. The collection was commissioned by the manufacturers, Spillers Foods, and they feature Arthur in different situations; scenes from the Arthur's ads and other events relevant to his status as a star! Arthur, incidentally, is a rescue cat discovered at the Wood Green Animal Shelter.

The Arthur the Cat Collection made its debut in January 1994 at the Scottish Cat Club Show. A special 'Arthur' Limited Edition, Arthur - First Class was available exclusively for those present at the show (and later via the Collectors Club) but did not enter the main collection (See 'Rare and Unreleased Items' section).

ARTHUR MAKES UP

Code: CA001
Issued: July 1994
Issue Price: £13.50

ARTHUR'S NIGHT HOME

Code: CA002
Issued: July 1994
Issue Price: £13.50

ARTHUR THE DIRECTOR

Behind the scene, Arthur ensures everything is going to plan.

Code: CA101
Issued: July 1994
Issue Price: £8.95

ARTHUR'S FIRST LESSON

Taking time out to give some good advice to the little ones.

Code: CA102
Issued: July 1994
Issue Price: £8.95

ARTHUR AND GEORGE

Arthur and a co-star from one of his ads.

Code: CA201
Issued: July 1994
Issue Price: £5.95

ARTHUR THE CAMERA CAT

Code: CA202
Issued: Feb 1995
Issue Price: £5.95

ARTHUR LEARNS HIS LINES

Code: CA301
Issued: July 1994
Issue Price: £4.25

ARTHUR'S TRAVELS

Code: CA302
Issued: July 1994
Issue Price: £4.25

A star's life is a busy one but now it's holiday time!

ARTHUR'S FAVOURITE

Code: CA303
Issued: July 1994
Issue Price: £4.25

ARTHUR'S FORTY WINKS

Code: CA304
Issued: July 1994
Issue Price: £4.25

GOOD GOLLY

A collection of antique gollies captured in miniature by Peter Fagan in a variety of activities. Gollies are traditionally the teddy bear's best friend and some of the figurines include teddies.

MARTHA THE MYSTIC

Code: GG001
Issued: July 1994
Issue Price: £14.95

PEANUT & CANDY'S PICNIC

Code: GG002
Issued: July 1994
Issue Price: £14.95

PUPPET ON A STRING

Code: GG003
Issued: July 1995
Issue Price: £14.95
No picture Available

GOLLY POPS HERE

Code: GG004
Issued: Feb 1995
Issue Price: £14.95

MOSES ROSES

Code: GG005
Issued: Feb 1995
Issue Price: £14.95

Other Items

103

Other Items

MARVO THE MAGNIFICO
Code: GG101
Issued: July 1994
Issue Price: £12.75

NIMBLE & THIMBLE
Code: GG102 
Issued: July 1994
Issue Price: £12.75

VINCENT VAN GOLLY
Code: GG103
Issued: July 1994
Issue Price: £12.75

IVOR ON THE IVORIES
Code: GG104
Issued: Feb 1995
Issue Price: £12.75

WHAT A PICTURE
Code: GG1045
Issued: July 1995
Issue Price: £12.75
No picture available

TOP BRASS
Code: GG201
Issued: July 1994
Issue Price: £8.95

MOJO
Code: GG202
Issued: July 1994
Issue Price: £8.95

BASS CLEF
Code: GG203
Issued: July 1994
Issue Price: £8.95

LICK THE STICK
Code: GG204
Issued: Feb 1995
Issue Price: £8.95

GOLLY GALLEON
Code: GG205 
Issued: Feb 1995
Issue Price: £8.95

MISS MOLLY
Code: GG206
Issued: Feb 1995
Issue Price: £8.95

GOLLY WHAT A SHOW
Code: GG207
Issued: July 1995
Issue Price: £8.95
(No picture available prior to publication)

GOLLY GEE UP
Code: GG208
Issued: July 1995
Issue Price: £8.95
(No picture available prior to publication)

BARCLAYCARD PROFILES

Sculptures by Peter Fagan are available to Barclaycard holders via their Profiles catalogue. Profiles is a loyalty scheme whereby points are accrued depending on the amount of purchases made using Barclaycard. Pieces from the current ranges of Teddies and Home Sweet Home are available (Story Time, Rabbit Hutch, On The Fence, Educating Timmy), and the option to purchase a year's membership to the Collectors Club. Barclaycard have also commissioned two pieces exclusively for their Profiles catalogue, Racing Ted and Cosy Kittens, between May 1994 and May 1995. Both pieces will join the Colour Box range and become available to all collectors in 1996.

Cosy Kittens
Issued: May 1994

Cosy Kittens does not have an issue price: Barclaycard holders require 600 Profile points to purchase this piece, and one point is awarded for every £10 charged on a Barclaycard.

COLOURWAYS

For a number of years prior to the introduction of special promotional pieces in 1993, Colour Box created colourways of figurines from the current collections for limited sale at store promotions and other events.

From left to right: Colourways of All Lit Up, Afternoon Stroll and Fireside Comfort.

Other Items

105

HOME SWEET HOME
Afternoon Stroll
(HS425)
Blue pram, pale green blanket, green/white striped ball — produced for Lynn's Cards and Gifts, Woking, Nov 1993.

All Lit Up
(HS626)
Red & green lampshade — produced for Lawleys, Reading, Oct 1993.

Bookworm
(HS610)
Pink and blue books — produced for Cameo House, Chesham, Jun 1994.

Fireside Comfort
(HS616)
'Brick' red/brown slipper — about 300 produced for Church's, Northampton, Sept 1992.

Inconvenience
(HS524)
Black cat, gold trimming and 'I'r Dim' on side of potty — produced for Just Right, Denbigh, Sept 1993.

Football Crazy
(HS532)
1) Green/white striped scarf (Hibs colours) — produced as a 'one-off' and presented to Keith Wright of the Hibernian Football Club at the launch of the Sick Kids Appeal, Sept 1991.
2) Maroon/white striped scarf (Hearts colours) — produced as a 'one-off' and presented to Scott Crabbe of the Heart of Midlothian Football Club at the same event as above.
3) Red/white striped scarf — produced for Owen Owen, Ilford, Oct 1992.

Just Good Friends
(HS534)
Blue edging round heart — presented as gifts to collectors who attended the Colour Box Collectors Club weekend at the Johnstoneburn House Hotel (not far from Lauder), April 1991.

Kettle
(HS612)
Yellow and sage green kettle — produced for Lawleys Collectors Weekend, Apr 1993.

Lots of Luck
(HS714)
Ginger cat — produced for Choice, Welwyn, Sept 1993.

Petal Puss
(HS711)
Pink flower with blue centre — produced for Cottage Crafts, Sawbridgeworth, Sept 1992.

Puss in Boots
(HS627)
Green wellingtons — produced for Glorious Britain, Gatwick Airport, Jul 1993.

Waterbed
(HS631)
Blue hot water bottle — produced for Randells, Wellingborough, Nov 1993.

PERSONALITY PUPS
Frankie
(DG211)
Blue slipper — produced for Lawleys Collectors Weekend, Apr 1993.

Frazer
(DG110)
Red and green football — produced for Lawleys, Reading, Oct 1993.

Peaceful Pup
(DG007)
Different coloured bow — produced for Cottage Crafts, Sawbridgeworth, Sept 1992.

PROMOTION PIECES

These pieces (three in all, one for each of the main collections) were specially designed to be painted with appropriate text as a souvenir of Colour Box promotions and replaced the idea of colourways of existing pieces. They are generally only available at a promotion, on the day, though retailers also mail out the pieces by prior arrangement if collectors cannot attend in person.

Certain detail on each piece is specially painted for each promotion and no two versions are alike. Colour Box give the shop hosting each promotion the opportunity to choose the colours of their own colourway.

PROMOTION PUP

Code No: SPP01
Issued: December 1993
Issue Price: £4.99

The ball is painted differently for each promotion.

TRAVELLING CAT

Launched at a promotion in Selfridges, London, on 25th September 1993. Travelling Cat's bow is painted differently for each promotion.

Code No: HSH02
Issued: September 1993
Issue Price: £6.50

POINT OF SALE BLACKBOARD

Code: CC87
Issued: March 1993
Issue Price: £7.99

Blackboard was originally issued back in 1984 as a point of sale for retailers to display in their shops. In those days, it had a second cat — Striped Cat (H1) — which was replaced by a teddy bear for relaunch in 1993. In its original form a version was also created for the USA using the transatlantic trading name 'Adorables'. Blackboard has had yet a further incarnation — as the free joining gift to members of the 1987 Collectors Club.

TABLEAUX

Issued: 1991
Edition Size: 1,000 of each (6,000 total).
Limited edition sculptured pictures designed to hang on the wall or stand on a table. Available in three styles: 1) In a free-standing unlit wooden frame [except Night Out and Tradesmans Entrance] (TU). 2) In a specially mounted light box with hand finished wooden surround (TL). 3) In a lit picture frame for wall mounting (TW). All wall versions were signed by Peter Fagan. A complete set were sold at the 1993 Christie's auction for £143.
Issue Prices: TU = £79; TL = £99; TW = £170

NIGHT OUT
Code: TL1 / TW1

TRADESMANS ENTRANCE
Code: TL2 / TW2

ON THE TILES
Code: TU3 / TL3 /TW3

NIGHT ON THE TILES
Code: TU4 / TL4 TW4

BACKYARD
Code: TU5 / TL5 / TW5

THE ATTIC
Code: TU6 / TL6 / TW6

ADDITIONAL ITEMS

CELEBRATION CAKES
Issued: 1986 Retired: 1987

Snowman, Yule Log, Christmas Star, Festive Ring, Gingerbread House

CAKE DECORATIONS
A set of cake decorations specially made in 1993 for and available only from John Lewis department stores.

MENUS
Issued: 1987 Retired: 1988

Sets of miniature food presented in a hamper-style box

Breakfast, Lunch, High Tea, Dinner, Wedding Breakfast, Christmas Dinner, Picnic Lunch

MINIATURE VILLAGE COLLECTION by John Clark
All pieces — Issued: 1987 Issue Price: £8.99 (except St Marys Church £10)
Retired: 1989 (except Rural Retreat, Farm Cottage and Suffolk Melford House Retired: 1988)
A collection of miniature buildings created by Colour Box's Creative Director. The first eleven pieces were styled The Miniature Village Collection and launched in 1987. Three were retired the following year and eight new ones issued. The entire range was then renamed Town and Country Collection and retired in 1989.

Regency Villa   Village Shop   St Marys Church
Brick House   Cotswold Cottage   Suffolk Melford House
Rural Retreat   The Angel Inn   Victorian Lodge House
Farm Cottage   Yeomans Farm House

TOWN AND COUNTRY COLLECTION by John Clark
All pieces — Issued: 1988 Retired: 1989 Issue Price: £10 (except Gothic Folly, Devon Thatched Weather Boarded House £8.99)

St Marys Church   Dale View   Regal Cinema
Gothic Folly   Palace Hotel   Seaside Georgian
Devon Thatched   Suburban Semi   Weather Boarded House

EARLY DAYS by Ann Shambrook
A collection of child figurines issued and retired in 1991.

Make a Wish
Code: EA001

Love For Me
Code: EA007

Derby Day
Code: EA013

Birthday Girl
Code: EA002

Tender Care
Code: EA008

Delightful Days
Code: EA014

Summer Days
Code: EA003

Billy The Kid
Code: EA009

Make Believe
Code: EA016

Evening Prayer
Code: EA004

Saucy Sioux
Code: EA010

Boyhood dreams
Code: EA017

Brunette Bouquet
Code: EA005

Blonde Bouquet
Code: EA011

Sleepy Time
Code: EA018

Nice Surprise
Code: EA006

Story Time
Code: EA012

Seasonal Collection

Since 1988 Peter Fagan has created a number of Christmas sculptures, often featuring characters from other collections in festive surroundings. Needless to say they are amongst the most popular of all Colour Box creations.

Code: XHS002
Issued: Sept 1991
Retired: 1992
Issue Price: £12

CHRISTMAS TIPPLE

Moved to Home Sweet Home as Drinks All Round (HS334). The name was changed so the piece would not be restricted to the Christmas market. Originally the wood on the cabinet was painted with darker shading around the edges, but this was changed to a single colour for ease of painting.

YULETIDE

About 100 were produced in 1987 (Mould 1), but production was stopped due to technical difficulties; the recessed back of the piece was a weak point and made the piece prone to breakage. When reissued two years later, the piece had been strengthened considerably by filling in the recess (Mould 2). The two versions are generally painted differently and also vary in detail in a number of ways: a teddy bear, Johann, replaces White Cat (H42) sitting next to the log basket; the year '1987' is missing from the Christmas Card hanging above the hearth; the year is also removed from the marking (© 1987 Peter Fagan / © Peter Fagan). Both versions have the inscription 'Santa's Little Helpers' — presumably a working title used prior to Yuletide. Because the recessed back was filled in for the later version, Mould 2 it is much heavier than Mould 1. Certain features on this piece also appear on Festive Fun (HS319).

Code: XHS014
Issued: 1987/9
Retired: 1991
Issue Price: £40 ('87)

Mould 1   Mould 2

109

CHRISTMAS PUDDING

Code: XHS217
Issued: 1989
Retired: 1991
Issue Price: £6

SNOWMAN

Code: XHS018
Issued: 1988
Retired: 1991
Issue Price: £30

Code: XHS019
Issued: 1989
Retired: 1991
Issue Price: £70

CHRISTMAS EVENING

The first 500 copies were signed by Peter Fagan as a promotion to launch their 1989 Christmas catalogue. However, the actual piece itself does not have a signature or date.

Seasonal Collection

Code: XHS020
Issued: 1990
Retired: 1993
Issue Price: £30

IS SANTA COMING?

This must be the question every child asks at some time as the Festive season approaches. There is always a special silence in the house on Christmas Eve and up on the roof we see some of Santa's most interested friends hoping he won't notice as he slides silently onto the resting snow. The cats seem as excited about the cold white blanket as they are about their expected visitor. But how is he going to get down the chimney?! This piece demonstrates the fine attention to detail which Peter Fagan applies to his work: every brick and tile was sculpted individually and then assembled just as a builder would construct a real chimney. Prior to launch, Is Santa Coming? revelled in the exciting working title of "Roof"!

Code: XHS024
Issued: 1991
Retired: 1993
Issue Price: £5

NUTCRACKER SUITE

Code: XHS023
Issued: 1991
Retired: 1993
Issue Price: £7

SANTA PAWS

Although retired in the UK a colourway was reintroduced in 1994 in the USA as part of the Pennywhistle Lane collection.

CHRISTMAS CAROLS

Reintroduced in 1994 in the USA as part of the Pennywhistle Lane collection.

Code: XHS025
Issued: 1992
Retired: 1993
Issue Price: £4.50

CHRISTMAS CRACKER CAT

Peter's cats all hate crackers but love the paper chaos afterwards and can't wait until all the bits of shining tinsel and paper tissue hats have landed on the floor. Then follows the game of paper chase as they rip everything up and try to put the little plastic cracker toys around the room. It is always chaotic after lunch in the Fagan household!

Code: XHS421
Issued: 1988
Retired: 1993
Issue Price: £4.50

Seasonal collection

Section Three

Rare & Unreleased Items

ARTHUR - FIRST CLASS
Issued: January 1994
Issue Price: £4.50

To commemorate the launch of the Arthur The Cat Collection at the Scottish Cat Club Show in January 1994, Peter sculpted a special piece, Arthur - First Class. The piece was only available at the show, although a number were also offered to Colour Box Collectors Club members thereafter via the Club newsletter on a first-come-first-served basis.

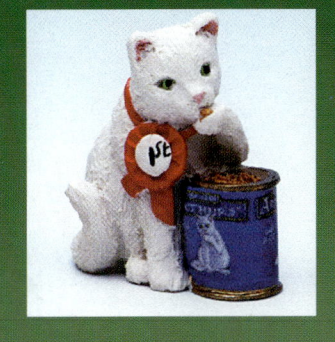

BABY ANIMALS
(1983-86)

A collection which initially preceded Colour Box, originated in bronze and then adapted for ceramic casting. These are rare and highly collectable, and even Colour Box don't have a complete set in their archive. A lot of three pieces (Hedgehog, Baby Owls and Fawn) plus nine cold cast bronze resin pieces were sold in the 1993 Christie's auction for £66.
Baby Owls, Baby Seal, Bear Cub, Badgers, Duckling, Fawn, Harvest Mice, Hedgehog, Kitten, Mouse, Panda, Squirrel.

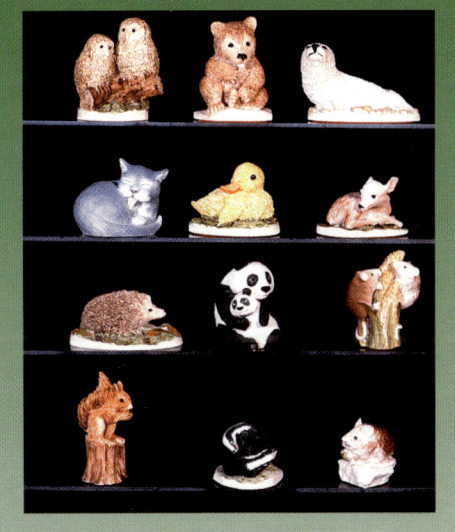

HUMPTY DUMPTY

This piece predates the Colour Box collection and, excluding private commissions and art sculptures, is one of the first pieces he ever made. Six pieces were cast from old moulds discovered in the loft of Peter's original workshop in Lauder, and offered as a lot in the 1993 Christie's auction. Three were in cold cast resin and three in hand painted ceramic resin.
1993 Auction Price: £176 (set of 6)

LUCKY FOR SOME

Peter's original design for Lots of Luck (HS714) had the horseshoe upside down (which actually brings bad luck), as this is how the old horseshoe is hammered on the door of his outside shed. Such was the consternation in the Colour Box design studio, however, that he agreed to remodel it the other way up. This, the original master, is unique and is the only Colour Box model ever to be sold without official design approval. It was included in the 1993 Christie's sale and, in conjunction with a conventional signed Lots of Luck, fetched £121.

'Lucky For Some' Lots of Luck

THE MUTTS
(1984-1987)

A collection of five mischievous mongrels (Mavis, Midge, Millie, Monty, Morris) and three locations for them (Bathtub Terror [not pictured here], Mutthouse Madness, Pavement Piazza). All the pieces were discontinued in 1987, but Bathtub Terror (the 'terror' being the Mutts' fear of bathtime) was resurrected in the same year for the Home Sweet Home Collection and renamed Bath Tub (then again in 1991 as Bath).

SPOTTY HOUND DOGS

A prototype collection of eight dogs which was never launched — Personality Pups arrived instead! These eight masters were sold at the Christie's auction.
1993 Auction Price: £88 (set)

WITCH AND DOG & KENNEL

As the concept of Colour Box was formulating in Peter Fagan's mind during the early 1980s he sculpted a number of bits and pieces — "just playing around with ideas." The witch did not come to anything, but the cat on her shoulder is clearly a Hopscotch prototype. The dog, too, found his way into the Hopscotch collection (H30) whilst the kennel developed into part of The Mutts in 1984. These pieces are still owned by Peter and Frances Fagan.

Rare & Unreleased

115

Memorabilia

This section includes details of some ranges which also include items relating to the Colour Box Teddy Bear Collection.

DISPLAY STANDS

A selection of display units have been created to complement the Home Sweet Home, Hopscotch and Miniature collections:

Pine House
Issued: 1983
Retired: 1986

Mahogany Shelf
Issued: 1983
Retired: 1986

Thatched Shelf
Issued: 1983
Retired: 1986

Tiled Shelf
Issued: 1983
Retired: 1986

Room Interiors
Issued: 1983
Retired: 1986
A selection of five assorted room backdrops.

Canopy House Display Shelf
Issued: 1989
Issue Price: £29.50
Perspex shelves in the shape of a house against a flat wall background to create room settings.

Colour Box have also produced a variety of cardboard point of sale material for all their ranges over the years available only to stockists.

BOOKS

THE HOME SWEET HOME COLLECTION
Code: BK005
Issued: 1991
Issue Price: £2.95
Features pictures of all the Home Sweet Home collection available at the time.

PICTURES

Commissioned portraits of some of the Teddies and Home Sweet Home Collections depicting scenes from their lives. The pictures are the work of artists Deidre Mackay-Clark (Teddies) and Julie Jones (Home Sweet Home). They are framed under glass in high-quality mounts. Three of them — Robert and Dickie, Jilly and Bernard, Bruno and Teddy Robinson — are signed limited editions.

Nursery Time
Code: PS11
Issued: 1990
Issue Price: £7.75

Shelf-life
Code: PS12
Issued: 1990
Issue Price: £7.75

The Listener
Code: PS13
Issued: 1990
Issue Price: £7.75

Washday Blues
Code: PS14
Issued: 1990
Issue Price: £7.75

Home Cooking
Code: PS15
Issued: 1990
Issue Price: £7.75

Festive Fun
Code: PS16
Issued: 1990
Issue Price: £7.75

Fishermans Friend
Code: PS17
Issued: 1990
Issue Price: £7.75

Theodore
Code: PS21
Issued: 1990
Issue Price: £12.99

Johann
Code: PS22
Issued: 1990
Issue Price: £12.99

Jonathan
Code: PS23
Issued: 1990
Issue Price: £12.99

The Listener
Code: PL13
Issued: 1990
Issue Price: £12.99

Washday Blues
Code: PL14
Issued: 1990
Issue Price: £12.99

Home Cooking
Code: PL15
Issued: 1990
Issue Price: £12.99

Fishermans Friend
Code: PL17
Issued: 1990
Issue Price: £12.99

Peregrine, Sopwith and Ralph
Code: PT001
Issued: July 1990
Issue Price: £14.99

Johann, Jonathan and Theodore
Code: PT002
Issued: July 1990
Issue Price: £14.99

Leftovers
Code: PS18
Issued: July 1990
Issue Price: £12.99

Party Capers
Code: PS19
Issued: July 1990
Issue Price: £12.99

Peregrine
Code: PS24
Issued: July 1990
Issue Price: £12.99

Ralph
Code: PS25
Issued: July 1990
Issue Price: £12.99

Sopwith
Code: PS26
Issued: 1990
Issue Price: £12.99

Christopher
Code: PS27
Issued: 1991
Issue Price: £13.75

Peter
Code: PS28
Issued: 1991
Issue Price: £13.75

Gustav von Bruin
Code: PS29
Issued: 1991
Issue Price: £13.75

Robert and Dickie
(Limited Edition)
Code: PEL1
Issued: 1990
Edition Size: 950
Issue Price: £39.95
All pictures in the edition are signed by the artist.

Jilly and Bernard
(Limited Edition)
Code: PEL2
Issued: July 1990
Edition Size: 999
Issue Price: £39.95
All pictures in the edition are signed by the artist.

Bruno and Teddy Robinson
(Limited Edition)
Code: PEL3
Issued: 1991
Issue Price: £39.95

CARDS

Greetings cards with designs based upon the 'Picture' illustrations by Julie Jones.
Issued: 1990

COLOUR BOX ANTICS
Issued: late 1991

Nursery Time
(CA201)

The Listeners
(CA202)

Washday Blues
(CA203)

Four Friends
(CA204)

Party Capers
(CA205)

Sitting Pretty
(CA206).

PEEPSHOW
Issued: late 1991

Festive Fun
(CA101)

Washday Blues
(CA103)

The Listeners
(CA105)

Home Cooking
(CA102)

Shelf Life
(CA104)

The Attic
(CA106)

SWEATSHIRTS AND TEE-SHIRTS

Issued: Spring 1990
Issue Price: £14.95 (Sweatshirt)/£7.50 (Tee-shirt).

Sweatshirts in navy blue (50%cotton 50% polyester)
Tee-shirts in white (100% cotton)
Both with the Colour Box logo printed on the front.
Available in three sizes — Small, Medium and Large.

CERAMICS

Fine bone china featuring Colour Box Cats and Bears. All items supplied in customised presentation boxes.

Nursery Set
Code: CB51
Issued: 1990
Issue Price: £17.50
Three piece set (bowl, plate, mug) depicting the cats playing with Lucy's rocking horse in the nursery.

Washday Set
Code: CB53
Issued: 1990
Issue Price: £17.50
Three piece set (bowl, plate, mug) depicting the cats working in the kitchen on washday.

Four Friends Set
Code: CB53
Issued: 1990
Issue Price: £17.50
Three piece set (bowl, plate, mug) — also sold separately — depicting the four bears from the Curios Shop surrounded by toys.

The Listener Mug
Code: CM4
Issued: 1991
Issue Price:

Sitting Pretty Mug
Code: CM5
Issued: 1991
Issue Price:

Party Capers Mug
Code: CM6
Issued: 1991
Issue Price:

LAPEL PINS

Issued: March 1994
Issue Price: £1.95
A Colour Box lapel pin featuring the Colour Box logo.

PENNYWHISTLE LANE BROOCH

An enamel brooch of the Pennywhistle Lane logo created by Fish Enterprises and available in either blue or terracotta.
Issued: 1994
Issue Price: £1.95
Fish Enterprises also produce other Colour Box items in fine enamel.

CALENDAR

A 1995 Calendar available exclusively for Collectors Club members and their friends, featuring hand-painted scenes by Linda Lovatt.
Issued: September 1994
Issue Price: £5.75

COLOUR BOX VIDEO

Issued: Dec 1994
Issue Price: £12.99
A 45 minute video featuring (amongst other things) how the miniatures are made, in-store promotions and painting demonstrations, Sopwith's solo flight, the 1993 Christie's auction, and Colour Box staff and collectors.

GRUMBRIDGE

The familiar Home Sweet Home settings in gift tinware.

PERSPECTIVE PHOTOGRAPHICS

A range of colour postcards, depicting the original plush Colour Box Bears with stories on the reverse of each card to introduce the teddy characters.
Issue Price of all three sets: £9.95

Set No.1
Issued: September 1992
16 Postcards of Colour Box Teddies presented in a red silk wallet. Sets available to Collectors Club members included a message from Peter on the reverse of one of the cards.

Set No.2
Issued: March 1993
A further set of 16 Postcards featuring different Colour Box Teddies, this time in a yellow silk wallet.

Set No.3
Issued: March 1994
Eight notecards with sepia photographs of real cats, with envelopes, presented in a wallet.

Secondary Market Price Guide

Listed here are the prices at which Colour Box pieces with a secondary market value originally sold when first released in the UK (First Issue Price) and an estimate of their current values on the secondary market. First Issue Prices from 1992 onwards are based on Colour Box's Recommended Retail Price Lists; prior to 1991, retailers set their own prices and these have been reconstructed approximately from details of Colour Box's trade prices. Current valuations are quoted both in UK pounds and US dollars using an exchange rate of 1.6 dollars to the pound.

It must be stressed that the valuations given are intended as a guide only and should be regarded as such. They have been compiled by the publishers and are current at the time of publication. Their sources include information gleaned from collectors and dealers whenever possible, and elsewhere by taking details of availability prior to retirement into consideration.

Collectors selling to dealers should be prepared to deduct anything from 15% to 50% from the prices quoted — 40% is probably an acceptable working average. Higher prices are paid for pieces in perfect condition and in their original box with accompanying leaflets.

Bronze Age Limited wish to point out that in line with their policy of non-involvement in secondary market, the prices quoted in this book were researched solely by the publishers.

NAME	CODE	ISSUE DATE	FIRST ISSUE PRICE £	CURRENT VALUE £ / $
HOME SWEET HOME				
RABBIT HUTCH	HS012	1991	30.00	75-85 / 120-135
STAGE DOOR	HS011	1991	45.00	125-150 / 200-240
WHEELBARROW	HS014	1990	30.00	70-80 / 115-130
POTTING SHED	HS015	1987	20.00	50-60 / 80-95
COAL HOLE	HS017	1988	22.00	50-60 / 80-95
ON THE FENCE	(X)HS021	1991	30.00	50-60 / 80-95
KITCHEN RANGE	HS110	1984	14.00	35-45 / 55-75
WASHBASIN	HS112	1986	14.00	50-60 / 80-95
THE BREAKFAST TABLE	HS113	1987	14.00	
Pink tablecloth/ no grey cat				70-80 / 115-130
Green tablecloth/ grey cat				45-55 / 75-90
WASH TUB	HS114	1987	14.00	45-55 / 75-90
HIGH CHAIR	HS116	1989	11.00	40-50 / 65-80
TALLBOY	HS117	1989	15.00	40-50 / 65-80
THE SECRETARY	HS118	1990	19.00	
Brown desk				50-60 / 80-95
Cream desk				40-50 / 65-80
BRING ON THE CLOWNS	HS119	1990	12.00	35-45 / 55-75
WELSH DRESSER	HS211	1983	10.00	35-45 / 55-75
KITCHEN SINK CAT (Old Stone Sink)	HS212	1983	10.00	30-40 / 50-65
WASHSTAND	HS213	1989	11.00	35-45 / 55-75
BATH TUB	HS214	1987	12.00	35-45 / 55-75
GAS STOVE	HS215	1986	12.00	45-65 / 75-100

NAME	CODE	ISSUE DATE	FIRST ISSUE PRICE £	CURRENT VALUE £ $
SCHOOL DAYS	HS216	1987	12.00	35-45 / 55-75
DAYBREAK	HS311	1987	7.00	35-45 / 55-75
GANG'S CHAIR	HS312	1983	7.00	
Blue/Pink				25-35 / 40-55
Grey				15-25 / 25-40
SIDEBOARD	HS313	1984	7.00	30-40 / 50-65
CLOCK-WATCHER	HS315	1984	7.00	25-35 / 40-55
TOOL BOX	HS316	1987	9.00	25-35 / 40-55
GRAMOPHONE	HS317	1987	9.00	25-35 / 40-55
GOURMET CAT	HS318	1987	8.00	30-40 / 50-65
FESTIVE FUN	HS319	1987	8.00	45-55 / 75-90
EASTER BONNET	HS320	1988	5.00	25-30 / 40-50
DRESSING UP	HS321	1988	6.50	35-40 / 55-65
THE EPICURE	HS322	1988	6.50	20-30 / 35-50
TAKE THE BISCUIT	HS333	1990	10.00	25-35 / 40-55
DRINKS ALL ROUND	HS334	1992	12.00	35-45 / 55-75
SOLO'S CHAIR	HS410	1983	6.00	
Brown				80-100 / 130-160
Blue/Pink				35-45 / 50-75
THE LISTENER	HS411	1984	5.00	30-40 / 50-65
WASHDAY	HS413	1986	5.00	
Mould 1 (white cloth)				45-55 / 75-90
Mould 2 (spotted cloth)				30-40 / 50-65
BIRD TABLE	HS414	1986	5.00	35-40 / 55-65
BARREL	HS415	1986	5.00	35-45 / 55-75
GLADSTONE BAG	HS416	1987	8.00	30-35 / 50-55
A STITCH IN TIME	HS417	1987	5.00	25-30 / 40-50
WATERING CAN	HS418	1987	5.00	30-35 / 50-55
TRAVELLER	HS419	1987	10.00	
Brown trunk				40-50 / 65-80
White trunk				25-35 / 40-55
BIRTHDAY TREAT	HS420	1987	10.00	20-25 / 35-40
SUPPERTIME	HS422	1990	8.00	20-25 / 35-40
TUTTI FRUTTI	HS423	1990	8.00	20-25 / 35-40
LICK AND PROMISE	HS424	1990	8.00	20-25 / 35-40
THE GROUNDSMAN	HS434	1992	10.00	25-30 / 40-50
VACANT CHAIR	HS510	1983	5.00	
Brown				80-90 / 130-145
Blue/Pink				40-50 / 65-80
CATS' CRADLE	HS511	1986	6.00	
Brown cradle				40-50 / 65-80
White cradle				25-35 / 40-55
LAUNDRY LAYABOUT	HS512	1986	8.00	30-35 / 50-55
TRASH CAN CAT	HS514	1983	5.00	30-35 / 50-55
LAMP	HS516	1987	5.00	45-55 / 75-90
LUNCH BOX	HS517	1987	5.00	25-35 / 40-55
PACKING CAT	HS518	1987	5.00	25-30 / 40-50
FIRESIDE FRIEND	HS519	1987	5.00	25-30 / 40-50
THE ARTIST	HS520	1990	5.00	30-40 / 50-65
HOME COOKING	HS522	1990	5.00	30-35 / 50-55
GONE FISHING	HS523	1990	7.00	15-20 / 25-35

NAME	CODE	ISSUE DATE	FIRST ISSUE PRICE £	CURRENT VALUE £ $
INCONVENIENCE	HS524	1991	4.50	15-20 / 25-35
CHAMBERMAID	HS525	1991	5.00	15-20 / 25-35
COMFY CAT	HS526	1991	5.00	15-20 / 25-35
SIXPENNY CORNET	HS528	1991	5.00	15-20 / 25-35
FISH SUPPER	HS530	1991	8.00	25-35 / 40-55
FIRST FORMER	HS531	1991	8.00	25-35 / 40-55
FOOTBALL CRAZY	HS532	1991	8.00	25-35 / 40-55
RIGHT ON TIME	HS533	1991	8.00	15-25 / 25-40
KISS IT BETTER	HS535	1991	8.00	
Red Cross				50-60 / 80-95
Green Cross				20-30 / 35-50
BEACH BOY	HS536	1991	8.00	25-35 / 40-55
THE DECORATOR	HS537	1991	8.00	25-35 / 40-55
THE BUSKER	HS539	1991	8.00	15-20 / 25-35
THE DAILY GRIND	HS543	1992	8.00	15-20 / 25-35
KNIT ONE PURL ONE	HS544	1992	8.00	25-30 / 40-50
THE OPPORTUNIST	HS609	1988	5.00	15-20 / 25-35
CAT BASKET	HS611	1983	4.00	
Cream				45-55 / 75-90
Brown				25-35 / 40-55
KETTLE	HS612	1984	5.00	15-20 / 25-35
COAL SKUTTLE	HS613	1983	4.00	30-40 / 50-65
BOOT	HS614	1988	5.00	25-35 / 40-55
FLAT CAP	HS615	1987	4.00	25-30 / 40-50
FIRESIDE COMFORT	HS616	1988	5.00	20-30 / 35-50
WEE WILLIE WINKIE	HS617	1988	5.00	25-35 / 40-55
THE TROMBONIST	HS618	1989	8.00	25-35 / 40-55
TOP HAT CAT	HS619	1989	5.00	55-65 / 90-100
ONE FOR THE POT	HS619	1992	5.00	15-20 / 25-35
PIANO STOOL	HS620	1989	5.00	35-40 / 55-65
FLOWER POWER	HS621	1989	5.00	25-35 / 40-55
PASTRY COOK	HS621	1992	5.00	15-20 / 25-35
DUSTPAN PUSS	HS622	1989	5.00	25-35 / 40-55
FLAT CAT	HS622	1992	5.00	15-20 / 25-35
KATY'S BASKET	HS623	1989	8.00	30-40 / 50-65
ROCKING HORSE	HS625	1989	15.00	50-60 / 80-95
SINGING CAT	HS701	1992	1.75	10-15 / 15-25
CAT & WOOL	HS702	1992	1.75	10-15 / 15-25
CAT & FISHBONE	HS703	1992	1.75	10-15 / 15-25
CAT & TOY MOUSE	HS704	1992	1.75	10-15 / 15-25
CAT & BOW	HS705	1992	1.75	15-20 / 25-35
CAT & BALL	HS706	1992	1.75	15-20 / 25-35
MOUSE TRAP	HS802	1990	8.00	25-30 / 40-50
BREADBOARD	HS801	1990	8.00	25-30 /40-50
HIGH NOON	None	1983	7.00	80-100 / 130-160
MIDNIGHT CAT	None	1983	7.00	80-100 / 130-160
DOORSTOP DILEMMA	None	1984	10.00	100-125 / 160-200
WINDOW	None	1986	7.00	120-135 / 190-230
THE WALL	None	1983	6.00	80-100 / 130-160
Original version with Cat and Dove				

Secondary Market Price Guide

NAME	CODE	ISSUE DATE	FIRST ISSUE PRICE £	CURRENT VALUE £ $
COLLECTORS CLUB/ LIMITED EDITIONS				
BLACKBOARD	CC87	1987	Nil	60-70 / 95-115
EASEL	None	1988	Nil	60-70 / 95-115
ATTIC	None	1989	Nil	60-70 / 95-115
NOTICE BOARD	None	1990	Nil	55-65 / 90-100
WALL	None	1991	Nil	40-50 / 65-80
CHALKBOARD	None	1992	Nil	40-50 / 65-80
BILLBOARD	None	1993	Nil	30-40 / 50-65
DECORATIVE CAT	None	1988	12.00	75-85 / 120-135
SILVER MINIATURES		1989		
Mini Teddy			42.00	90-100 / 145-160
Cat & Ball	(H56)		50.00	90-100 / 145-160
MOTHER'S PRIDE	None	1991	12.00	40-50 / 65-80
DRESSING TABLE	None	1991	13.00	30-40 / 50-65
PICNIC PUSS	None	1992	20.00	50-70 / 80-115
DOLLS HOUSE	CC930S	1993	24.99	55-65 / 90-100
LAUNDRY PUPS	CC932S	1993	19.99	40-45 / 65-75
PRIVATE ENTRANCE	CC933S	1994	50.00	75-100 / 120-160
FESTIVE HOPSCOTCH (Set of 18 pieces)	None	1990	18.00	300-350 / 480-560
SEASONAL COLLECTION				
SNOWMAN	XHS018	1988	30.00	80-100 / 130-160
XMAS CRACKER CAT	XHS421	1988	4.50	20-30 / 35-50
CHRISTMAS EVENING	XHS019	1989	70.00	150-200 / 240-320
YULETIDE	XHS014	1987/9	40.00	
Mould 1 (1987)				350-450 / 560-720
Mould 2 (1989)				150-200 / 240-320
CHRISTMAS PUDDING	XHS217	1989	6.00	30-40 / 50-65
IS SANTA COMING?	XHS020	1990	30.00	70-90 / 115-145
CHRISTMAS TIPPLE	XHS002	1991	12.00	35-45 / 55-75
NUTCRACKER SUITE	XHS023	1991	7.00	30-40 / 50-65
SANTA PAWS	XHS024	1991	5.00	30-40 / 50-65
CHRISTMAS CAROLS	XHS025	1992	4.50	15-25 / 25-40
HOPSCOTCH MINIS				
PLAIN CAT	H2	1983	1.00	3-5 / 5-8
DOG (Brown markings)	H5	1983	1.00	10-15 / 15-25
GOLDFISH	H7	1983	1.00	50-60 / 80-95
MONKEY	H7	1983	1.00	30-40 / 50-65
DOG (Black markings)	H9	1983	1.00	10-15 / 15-25
SHEEP	H11	1983	1.00	10-15 / 15-25
CAT ON BACK	H13	1983	1.00	10-15 / 15-25
CAMEL	H14	1983	1.00	20-30 / 35-50
FAWN	H14	1983	1.00	20-30 / 35-50
SNAKE	H16	1983	1.00	20-30 / 35-50
LION	H16	1983	1.00	30-40 / 50-65
DOG (On Back)	H17	1983	1.00	5-15 / 8-25
SQUIRREL	H19	1983	1.00	10-15 / 15-25
MOUSE	H20	1983	1.00	20-30 / 35-50
SEAL	H20	1983	1.00	15-20 / 25-35

NAME	CODE	ISSUE DATE	FIRST ISSUE PRICE £	CURRENT VALUE £ $
BROWN COW	H22	1983	1.00	20-30 / 35-50
DORMOUSE	H22	1983	1.00	20-30 / 35-50
CAT	H25	1983	1.00	5-15 / 8-25
DOVE	H26	1983	1.00	30-40 / 50-65
ROBIN	H26	1983	1.00	30-40 / 50-65
DOG	H27	1983	1.00	20-30 / 35-50
KOALA	H29	1983	1.00	50-60 / 80-95
DOG (Brown or Black)	H30	1983	1.00	20-30 / 35-50
GREY CAT	H31	1986	1.00	5-15 / 8-25
LADYBIRD	H32	1986	1.00	30-40 / 50-65
BUMBLE BEE	H32	1987	1.00	30-40 / 50-65
BADGER	H33	1986	1.00	10-15 / 15-25
PIG ON BACK	H34	1986	1.00	10-15 / 15-25
RECLINING PIG	H35	1986	1.00	10-15 / 15-25
RECLINING CAT	H36	1987	1.00	10-15 / 15-25
FRIGHTENED CAT	H37	1987	1.00	10-15 / 15-25
BEGGING CAT	H38	1987	1.00	10-15 / 15-25
WASHING CAT	H39	1987	1.00	10-15 / 15-25
GUINEA PIG	H41	1987	1.00	30-40 / 50-65
HAMSTER	H41	1988	1.00	20-30 / 35-50
WHITE CAT	H42	1987	1.00	30-40 / 50-65
BIG BLACK CAT	H42	1988	1.00	15-25 / 25-40
SHAGGY DOG	H43	1987	1.00	5-15 / 8-25
PENGUIN	H44	1989	1.15	15-20 / 25-35
COCKEREL	H45	1989	1.15	15-20 / 25-35
HEN	H46	1989	1.15	10-15 / 15-25
BLUE TIT	H47	1989	1.15	10-15 / 15-25
HEDGEHOG BEGGING	H48	1989	1.15	5-7 / 8-11
SQUIRREL	H49	1989	1.15	15-20 / 25-35
HARE	H50	1989	1.15	5-7 / 8-11
DUCKLING	H52	1989	1.15	3-5 / 5-8
BROWN BEAR	H54	1989	1.15	15-20 / 25-35
BADGER	H55	1989	1.15	15-20 / 25-35
CAT AND BALL	H56	1989	1.15	5-7 / 8-11
SCOTTIE (White or Black)	H57	1989	1.15	15-20 / 25-35
SHEEPDOG	H58	1989	1.15	5-7 / 8-11
SHETLAND PONY	H59	1989	1.15	3-5 / 5-8
LAMB	H60	1989	1.15	3-5 / 5-8
SINGING CAT	H61	1991	1.15	3-5 / 5-8
CAT AND WOOL	H62	1991	1.15	3-5 / 5-8
CAT AND FISHBONE	H63	1991	1.15	5-7 / 8-11
CAT AND TOY MOUSE	H64	1991	1.15	3-5 / 5-8
CAT AND BOW	H65	1991	1.15	5-7 / 8-11
GORILLA	H67	1992	1.15	5-10 / 8-15
SNAKES ALIVE	H69	1992	1.15	5-7 / 8-11
PANDA RECLINING	H74	1992	1.15	5-7 / 8-11
ALLIGATOR	H75	1992	1.15	5-7 / 8-11
MONKEY	H76	1992	1.15	5-7 / 8-11
LEOPARD	H78	1992	1.15	5-7 / 8-11
PATTY	H79	1993	1.15	5-7 / 8-11
DIMEY	H80	1993	1.15	5-7 / 8-11

NAME	CODE	ISSUE DATE	FIRST ISSUE PRICE £	CURRENT VALUE £ $
TYRO	H81	1993	1.15	5-7 / 8-11
PARRY	H82	1993	1.15	5-7 / 8-11
TRICEY	H83	1993	1.15	5-7 / 8-11
STEGGY	H84	1993	1.15	5-7 / 8-11
MR NOAH	H85	1993	1.15	5-7 / 8-11
MRS NOAH	H86	1993	1.15	5-7 / 8-11

MINIATURES
A complete set of the Miniature Collection (75 pieces) was auctioned at Christie's in 1993 and fetched 132.

NAME	CODE	ISSUE DATE	FIRST ISSUE PRICE £	CURRENT VALUE £ $
CALF	MC1	1983	2.00	10-15 / 15-25
CAT (AND MOUSE)	MC2	1983	2.00	10-15 / 15-25
DUCK	MC3	1983	2.00	10-15 / 15-25
HEDGHOGS	MC4	1983	2.00	10-15 / 15-25
HEN (AND CHICKS)	MC5	1983	2.00	15-20 / 25-35
SEAL (AND PUP)	MC6	1983	2.00	15-20 / 25-35
MOUSE (AND TOADSTOOL)	MC7	1983	2.00	10-15 / 15-25
OTTER	MC8	1983	2.00	15-20 / 25-35
OWL	MC9	1983	2.00	10-15 / 15-25
PIG (AND PIGLETS)	MC10	1983	2.00	10-15 / 15-25
PONY AND FOAL	MC11	1983	2.00	10-15 / 15-25
RABBITS	MC12	1983	2.00	10-15 / 15-25
LABRADORS	MC13	1983	2.00	30-40 / 50-65
SHEEP AND LAMB	MC14	1983	2.00	10-15 / 15-25
SQUIRREL	MC15	1983	2.00	15-20 / 25-35
ELEPHANT	MC16	1985	2.50	30-40 / 50-65
PENGUIN	MC17	1985	2.50	15-20 / 25-35
KOALA	MC18	1985	2.50	15-20 / 25-35
WOODMOUSE	MC19	1986	2.50	10-15 / 15-25
FOX	MC20	1986	2.50	15-20 / 25-35
BADGER	MC21	1986	2.50	15-20 / 25-35
FROG	MC22	1986	2.50	10-15 / 15-25
MOLE	MC23	1986	2.50	15-20 / 25-35
SADDLEBACK PIG	MC24	1986	2.50	10-15 / 15-25
DUCK AND DUCKLINGS	MC13	1987	2.50	10-15 / 15-25
PUFFIN	MC16	1987	2.50	15-20 / 25-35
DOE AND FAWN	MC18	1987	2.50	10-15 / 15-25
TORTOISE	MC25	1987	2.50	15-20 / 25-35
KOALA	MC26	1987	2.50	15-20 / 25-35
BORDER COLLIE	MC27	1987	2.50	10-15 / 15-25
BRACE OF PHEASANTS	MC28	1987	2.50	15-20 / 25-35
LEAPING SALMON	MC30	1987	2.50	15-20 / 25-35
GOLDEN EAGLE	MC29	1987	2.50	15-20 / 25-35
FIELDVOLE AND WREN	MC31	1989	3.00	10-15 / 15-25
RABBIT FAMILY	MC32	1989	3.00	10-15 / 15-25
ROBIN	MC33	1989	3.00	10-15 / 15-25
BARN OWL	MC34	1989	3.00	10-15 / 15-25
CAT AND KITTENS	MC35	1989	3.00	10-15 / 15-25
COCK AND HEN	MC36	1989	3.00	10-15 / 15-25

NAME	CODE	ISSUE DATE	FIRST ISSUE PRICE £	CURRENT VALUE £ / $
RED SQUIRREL	MC37	1989	3.00	10-15 / 15-25
PINE MARTINS	MC38	1989	3.00	10-15 / 15-25
FOX AND CUBS	MC39	1989	3.00	10-15 / 15-25
HIGHLAND COW & CALF	MC40	1989	3.00	10-15 / 15-25
STOAT	MC41	1989	3.00	10-15 / 15-25
HARE	MC42	1989	3.00	10-15 / 15-25
BADGER AND CUBS	MC43	1989	3.00	10-15 / 15-25
BLUE TITS	MC44	1989	3.00	10-15 / 15-25
KANGAROO	MC45	1989	3.00	10-15 / 15-25
KINGFISHER	MC46	1989	3.00	10-15 / 15-25
DORMOUSE	MC47	1989	3.00	10-15 / 15-25
OTTER	MC48	1989	3.00	10-15 / 15-25
SEAL	MC49	1989	3.00	10-15 / 15-25
SOAY RAM	MC50	1989	3.00	10-15 / 15-25
WILD CAT	MC51	1989	3.00	10-15 / 15-25
HARVEST MOUSE	MC52	1990	4.00	10-15 / 15-25
EUROPEAN OWL	MC53	1990	4.00	10-15 / 15-25
BULLFINCH	MC54	1990	4.00	10-15 / 15-25
WOODPECKER	MC55	1990	4.00	10-15 / 15-25
GREY SQUIRREL	MC56	1990	4.00	10-15 / 15-25
GINGER KITTENS	MC57	1990	4.00	10-15 / 15-25
GUN DOG	MC58	1990	4.00	10-15 / 15-25
RETRIEVER AND PUPS	MC59	1990	4.00	10-15 / 15-25
PERSONALITY PUPS				
PATRICK	DG001	1991	2.00	5-10 / 8-15
PATCH	DG002	1991	2.00	5-10 / 8-15
PENNY	DG004	1991	2.00	5-10 / 8-15
POLO	DG008	1991	2.00	8-12 / 13-20
POPPY	DG018	1991	2.00	8-12 / 13-20
PING PONG	DG019	1991	2.00	8-12 / 13-20
THE JUGGLER	DG103	1991	3.00	10-15 / 15-25
ROLY POLY	DG105	1991	3.00	10-15 / 15-25
ROUGH AND TUMBLE	DG106	1991	3.00	8-12 / 13-20
PLAYTIME	DG107	1991	3.00	8-12 / 13-20
TICKLISH PUP	DG204	1991	4.50	10-15 / 15-25
FATHERLY LOVE	DG205	1991	4.50	10-15 / 15-25
OOPS A DAISY	DG206	1991	4.50	10-15 / 15-25

Index

Home Sweet Home Pieces only listed individually

AFTERNOON STROLL	33	CAT & WOOL	51	FAST MOVER	49
ALI-BABA	33	CAT CALL	41	FELINE FROLICS	97
ALL LIT UP	47	CAT FISH	54	FESTIVE FUN	29
ARTHUR THE CAT		CAT NAPPER	55	FIRE ENGINE	42
COLLECTION	102	CAT'S CHORUS	31	FIRESIDE COMFORT	44
THE ARTIST	36	CATS' CRADLE	35	FIRESIDE FRIEND	36
BAGPUSS	52	CENTRE FOLD	38	FIRST FORMER	38
BALLOON RACE	52	CHALKBOARD	96	FISH SUPPER	38
BARREL	31	CHAMBERMAID	37	FLAT CAP	44
BATH	40	CHIMNEY SWEEP	24	FLAT CAT	47
BATH TUB	26	CHRISTMAS CAROLS	111	FLOWER POWER	46
BATHTIME PAL	52	CHRISTMAS CRACKER CAT	111	FOOTBALL CRAZY	38
BEACH BOY	39	CHRISTMAS EVENING	110	*FROU-FROU COLLECTION*	64
BE MY VALENTINE	42	CHRISTMAS PUDDING	110	GANGS CHAIR	27
BEDSTEAD	24	CHRISTMAS TIPPLE	109	GAS STOVE	26
BEST VINTAGE	18	CLOCK-WATCHER	28	GIFT WRAP CAT	42
BEST WISHES CAT	50	THE COAL HOLE	21	GLADSTONE BAG	31
BIG SPENDER	48	COAL SKUTTLE	44	GLASS ALLEY CAT	52
BILLBOARD	96	COMFY CAT	37	GONE FISHING	37
BIN STEALING	34	CONGRATULATIONS		*GOOD GOLLY*	
BIRD SANCTUARY	30	CARD CAT	50	*COLLECTION*	103
BIRD TABLE	31	THE CORRESPONDENT	41	GOURMET CAT	28
BIRTHDAY CARD CAT	50	COSY KITTENS	105	GRAMOPHONE	28
BIRTHDAY TREAT	32	COSY TOES	55	GRANNY'S DRESSER	19
BLACKBOARD	95	THE DAILY GRIND	41	GRANNY'S KITCHEN	55
BOOKWORM	43	DAYBREAK	27	THE GROUNDSMAN	33
BOOT	44	DECORATIVE CAT	97	HEAD GARDENER	99
BOWLED OVER	42	THE DECORATOR	40	THE HEN HOUSE	19
BREADBOARD	54	DIG & DELVE	48	HIGH CHAIR	23
THE BRICKIE	49	DOG'S DINNER	54	HIGH NOON	56
THE BREAKFAST TABLE	23	DOLLS HOUSE	98	HIGH TIME	34
BRIGHT & EARLY	29	DOORSTEP DILEMMA	57	HOME COOKING	37
BRING ON THE CLOWNS	24	DRESSING UP	29	HOME SWEET HOME WALL	18
BRUSH UP	54	DRINKS ALL ROUND	30	*HOPSCOTCH COLLECTION*	72
BUILDERS' MATE	34	DUSTPAN PUSS	46	INCONVENIENCE	37
THE BUSKER	40	EARLY BLOOMERS	33	IS SANTA COMING?	111
BUTTERFLY CAT	52	EARLY RISER	48	JUST GOOD FRIENDS	39
CADDY CAT	26	EASEL	95	KATY'S BASKET	47
CAT & BALL	51	EASTER BONNET	29	KETTLE	43
CAT BASKET	43	EASTER SURPRISE	54	KISS IT BETTER	39
CAT & BOW	51	THE EPICURE	29	KISS ME QUICK	48
CAT & FISHBONE	51	THE EXECUTIVE	43	KITCHEN RANGE	22
CAT & TOY MOUSE	51	EXTRA PINT	47	KITCHEN SINK CAT	25

127

KNIT ONE PURL ONE	41	PRIMA BALLERINA	38	WASHSTAND	25
LAMP	36	PRIVATE ENTRANCE	99	WATCH THE BIRDIE	42
THE LAST DROP	34	PUSS IN BOOTS	48	WATERBED	48
LAUNDRY LAYABOUT	35	RABBIT HUTCH	19	WATERING CAN	32
LEARNER DRIVER	97	RIGHT ON TIME	39	WEE WILLIE WINKIE	44
LIBRARIAN	28	ROCKING HORSE	47	WEIGHING IN	49
LICK AND PROMISE	33	SANTA PAWS	111	WELSH DRESSER	25
LIGHTING UP TIME	50	SCHOOL DAYS	26	THE WHEELBARROW	20
THE LISTENER	30	THE SECRETARY	24	WINDOW	58
LITTLE SAVER	49	SHIPMATE	42	WINTER SPORT	34
LITTLE SPRINKLER	48	SIDEBOARD	27	WISHING WELL	55
LOTS OF LUCK	53	SINGING CAT	50	YULETIDE	109
LUCKY FOR SOME	114	SIXPENNY CORNET	38		
LUNCH BOX	36	SNOWMAN	110		
MIDNIGHT CAT	57	THE SOFA	21		
MILK CHURNS	18	SOLO'S CHAIR	30		
MILKMAID	53	STAGE DOOR	19		
MINIATURE COLLECTION	66	A STITCH IN TIME	32		
MOONLIGHT SERENADE	100	STOKE IT UP	46		
MOSES BASKET	40	STOOL PIGEON	49		
MOTHER'S PRIDE	98	SUPPERTIME	32		
MOUSE TRAP	54	*TABLEAUX*	107		
MUMMY'S BOY	53	TAKE THE BISCUIT	30		
MUMMY'S GIRL	53	TAKEAWAY	37		
THE MUSIC OF THE		TALLBOY	23		
POLYPHON	101	TASTY MORSEL	53		
NICE 'N' COSY	40	TEACHER'S PET	41		
NOTICE BOARD	96	THOROUGHBRED	34		
NUTCRACKER SUITE	111	TOILET	22		
(OLD) FIREPLACE	26	TOOL BOX	28		
ON THE FENCE	21	TOP CAT	54		
ONE FOR THE POT	45	TOP HAT CAT	45		
OPENING NIGHT	97	*TOWN AND COUNTRY*			
THE OPPORTUNIST	43	*COLLECTION*	108		
THE OUTSIDE PRIVY	20	TRASH CAN CAT	35		
PACKING CAT	36	TRAVELLER	32		
PASTRY COOK	46	TRAVELLING CAT	107		
PENNYWHISTLE LANE	82	THE TROMBONIST	45		
PERSONALITY PUPS	59	TUTTI FRUTTI	32		
PETAL PUSS	52	UPSTAIRS, DOWNSTAIRS	55		
PIANO POPS	25	VACANT CHAIR	35		
PIANO STOOL	45	WAKEY, WAKEY	55		
PICNIC PUSS	98	WALL	58		
PING PONG PUSS	52	THE WARDEN	50		
POP TO THE SHOP	49	THE WARDROBE	21		
PORKER PUSS	49	WASH TUB	23		
POST BOX	26	WASHDAY	31		
THE POTTING SHED	20	WASHBASIN	22		